Hues of Happiness

40 prints to inspire joy and creativity

Illustrated by: Danielle Di Stefano

Printed in the United States of America

First Edition

ISBN-10: 0692791795
ISBN-13: 978-0692791790 (Lirica Publications)

Cover by Danielle Di Stefano

Lirica Publications
P.O. Box 219
Eden, NY 14057

www.liricapublications.com
info@liricapublications.com

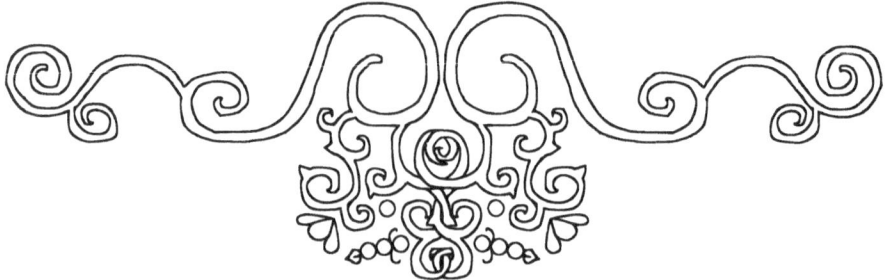

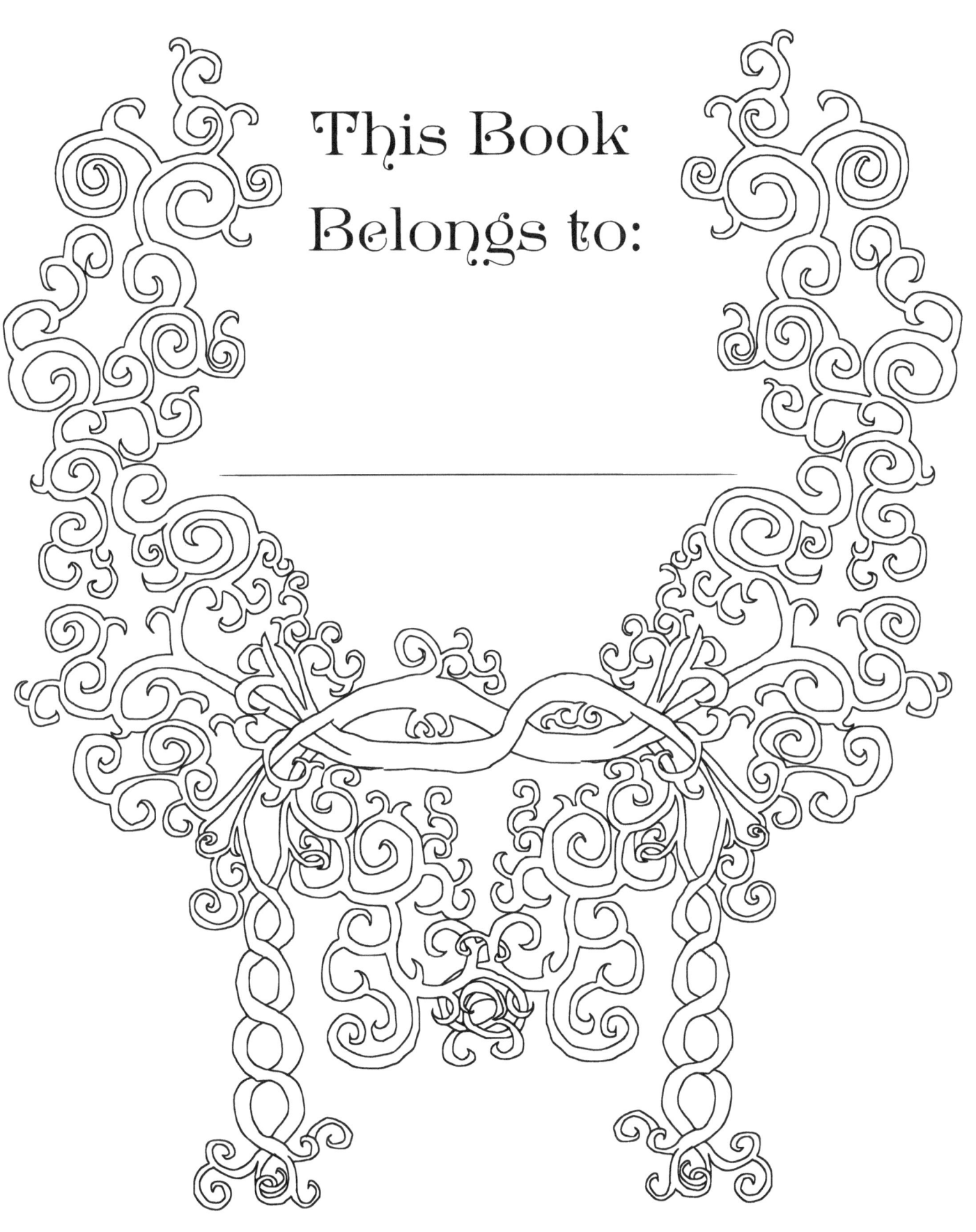

This Book
Belongs to:

About the Book

This book has been carefully hand-drawn with love. It is my intention that each work reflects the culture from which it draws inspiration. You'll notice influence from Celtic knotwork, Mughal paintings, mehndi (henna) designs, and Nordic carvings. While the subject matter varies, they are united by this unique, global aesthetic.

It is my sincere wish that this book brings much joy and relaxation. Put on your favorite music, break out your colored pencils and markers, and unleash your creativity.

Best of luck on your colorful journey!

About the Illustrator

Ms. Di Stefano is a soprano by trade, and a self-taught artist. As a published author, her articles have been featured in various opera-related publications. Her busy schedule includes performing, teaching music appreciation classes, illustrating, and caring for her adorable rescue puppy and kitten.

Her vast repertoire, spanning 16 languages and featuring both traditional and classical music, has greatly influenced her drawing style, as her illustrations embrace the beauty and charm of different cultures.

Ms. Di Stefano is excited to continue sharing her advocacy and love of the arts... be it on the stage, in a lecture hall, or through her coloring books.

Color Test Page

Mix, match, blend, and explore colors here!

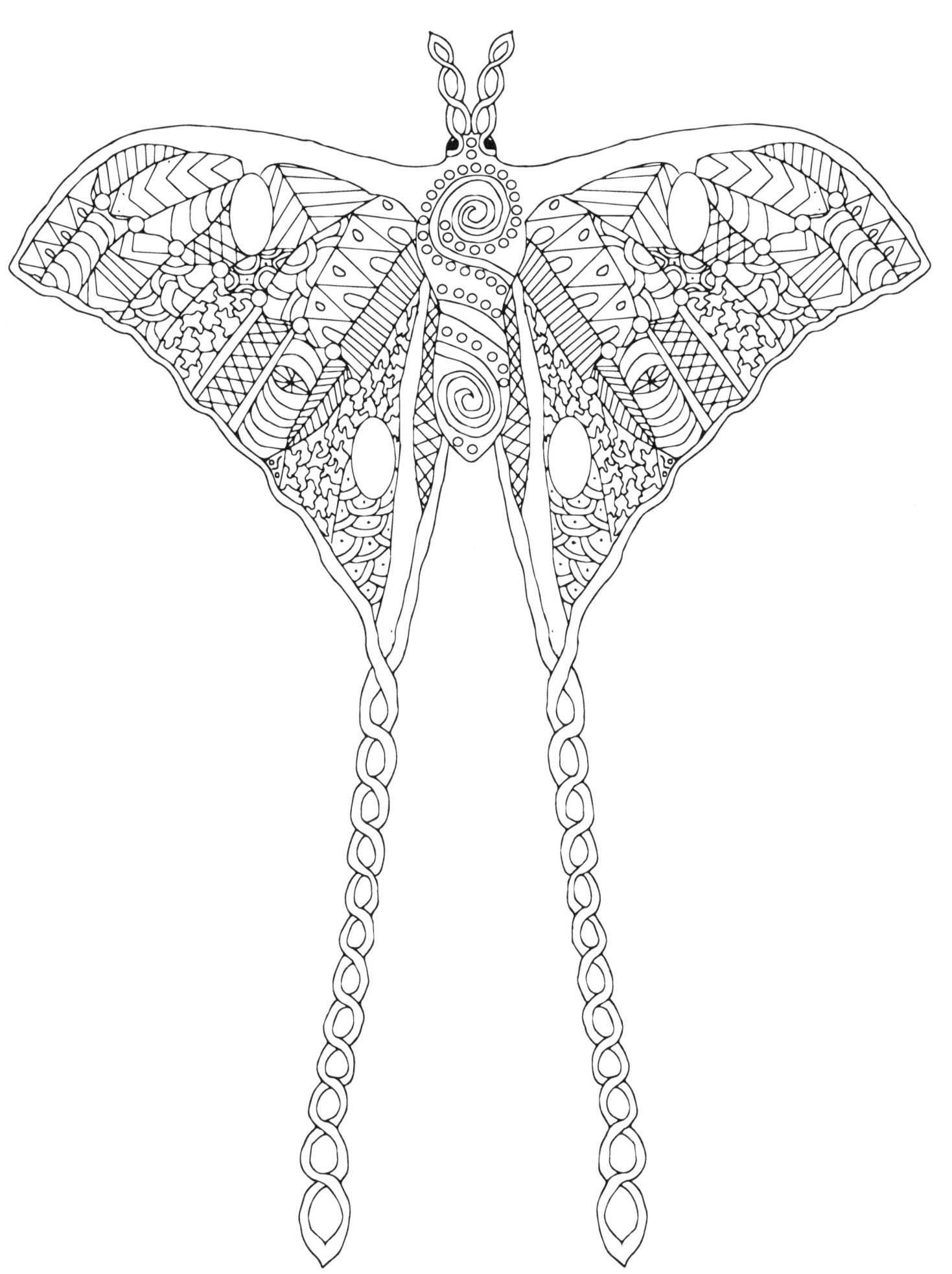

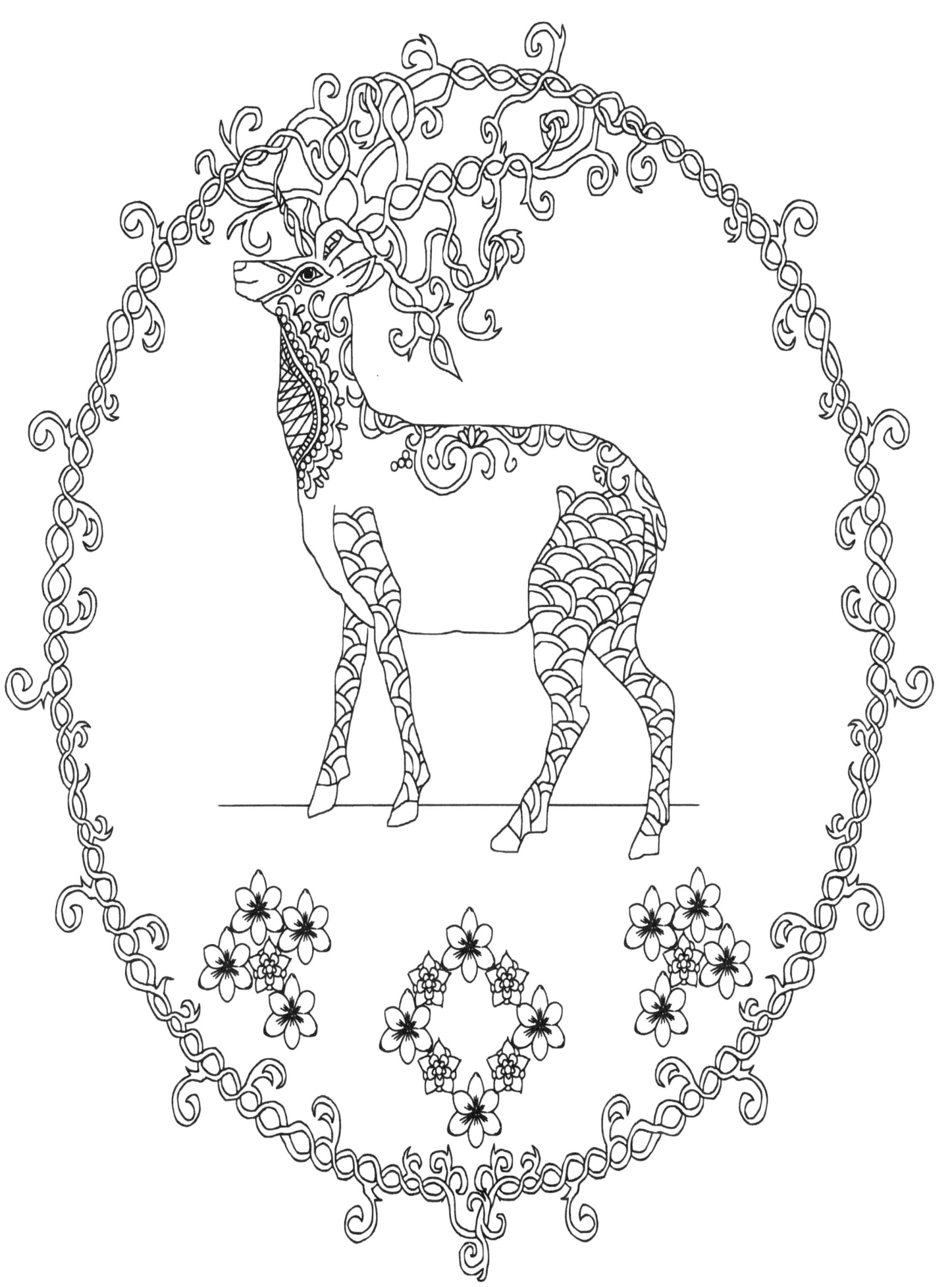

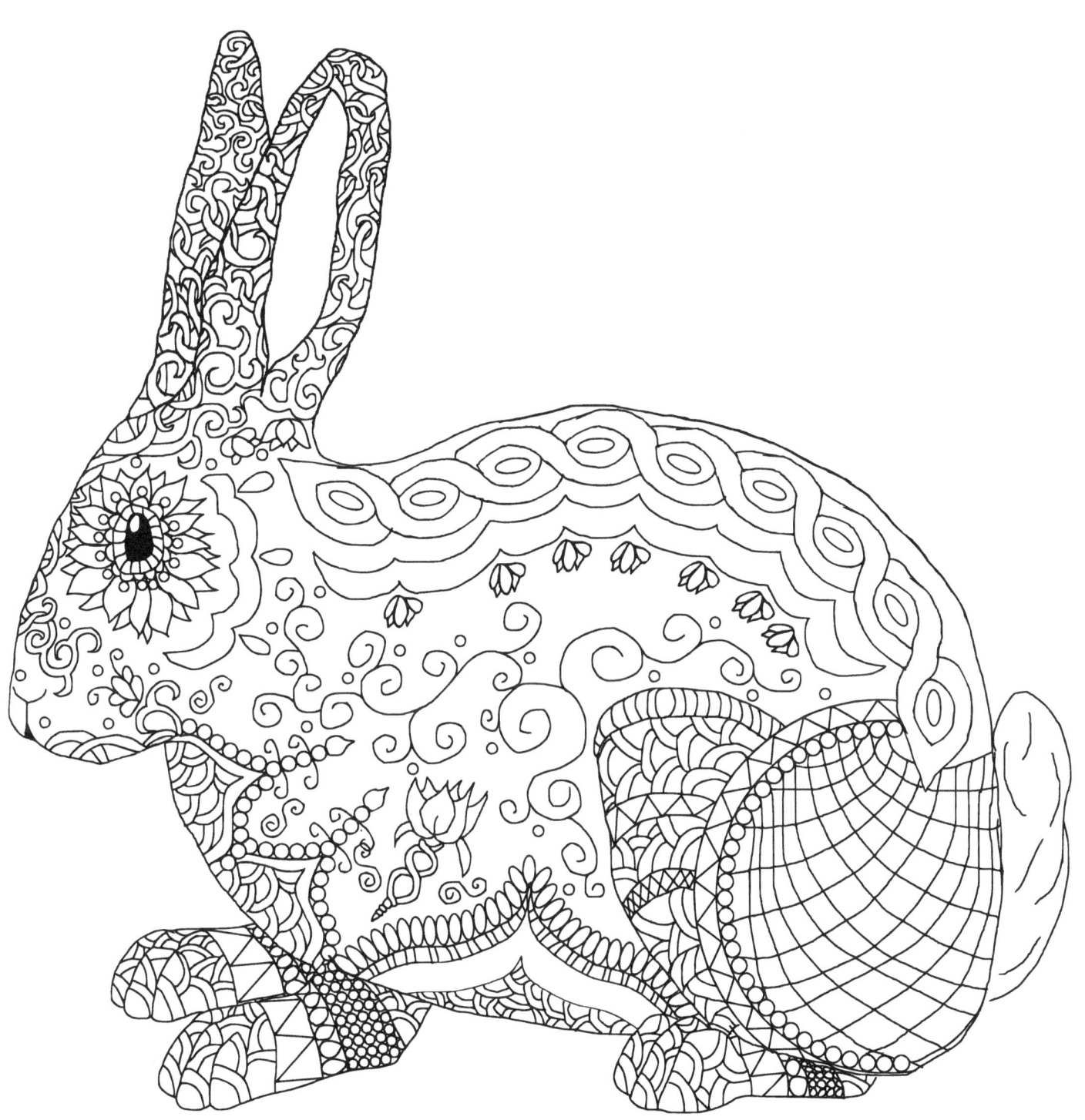

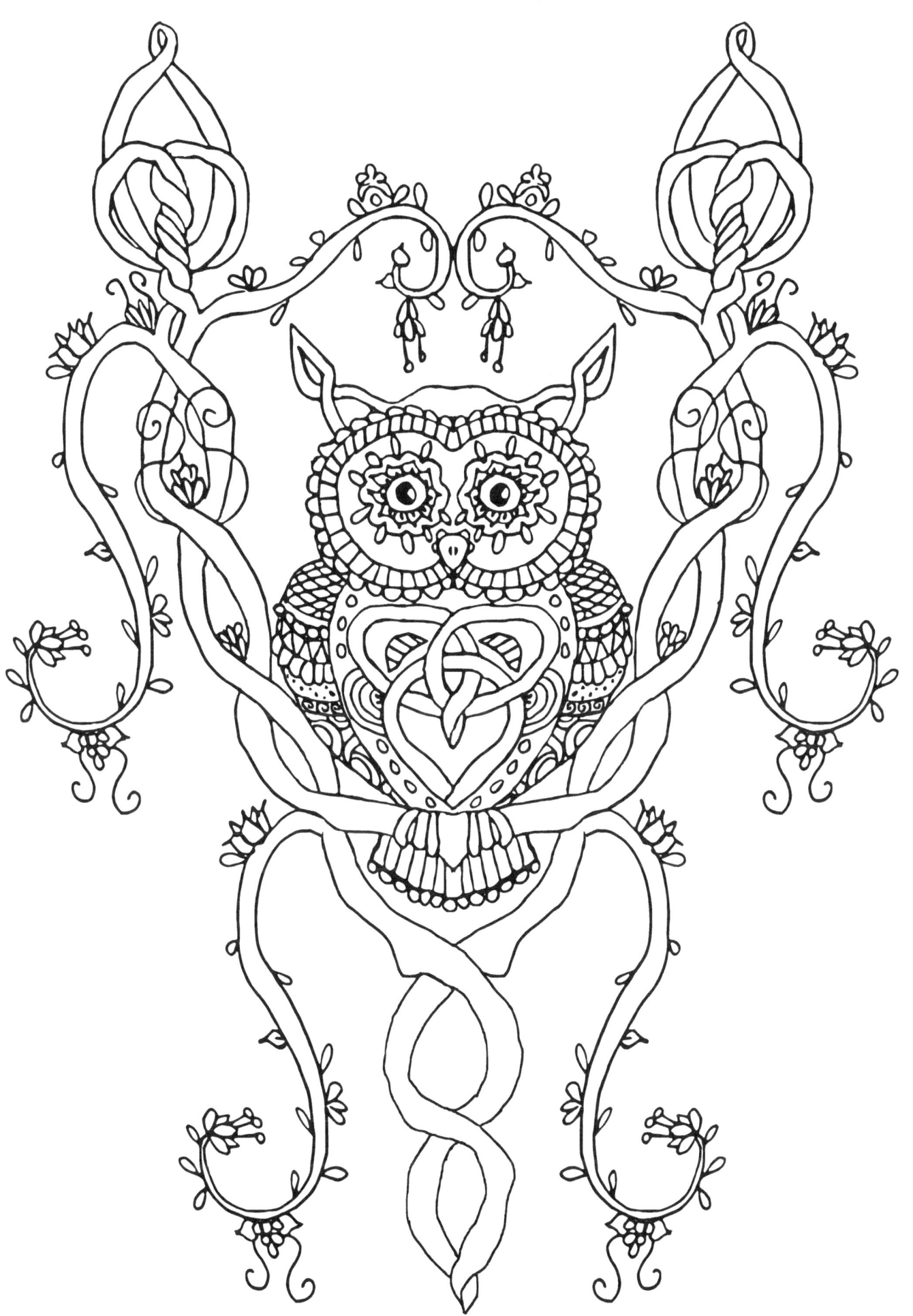

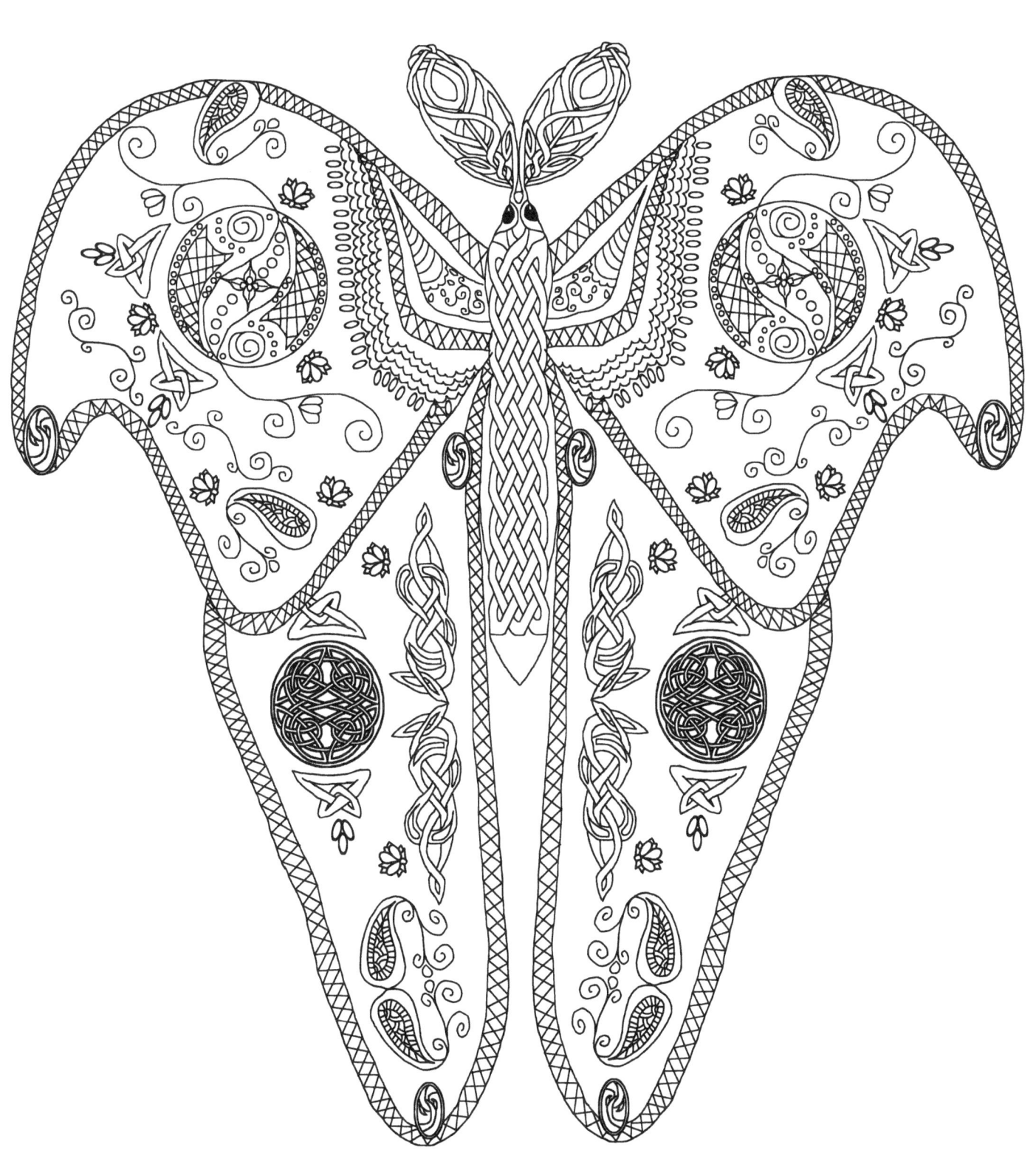

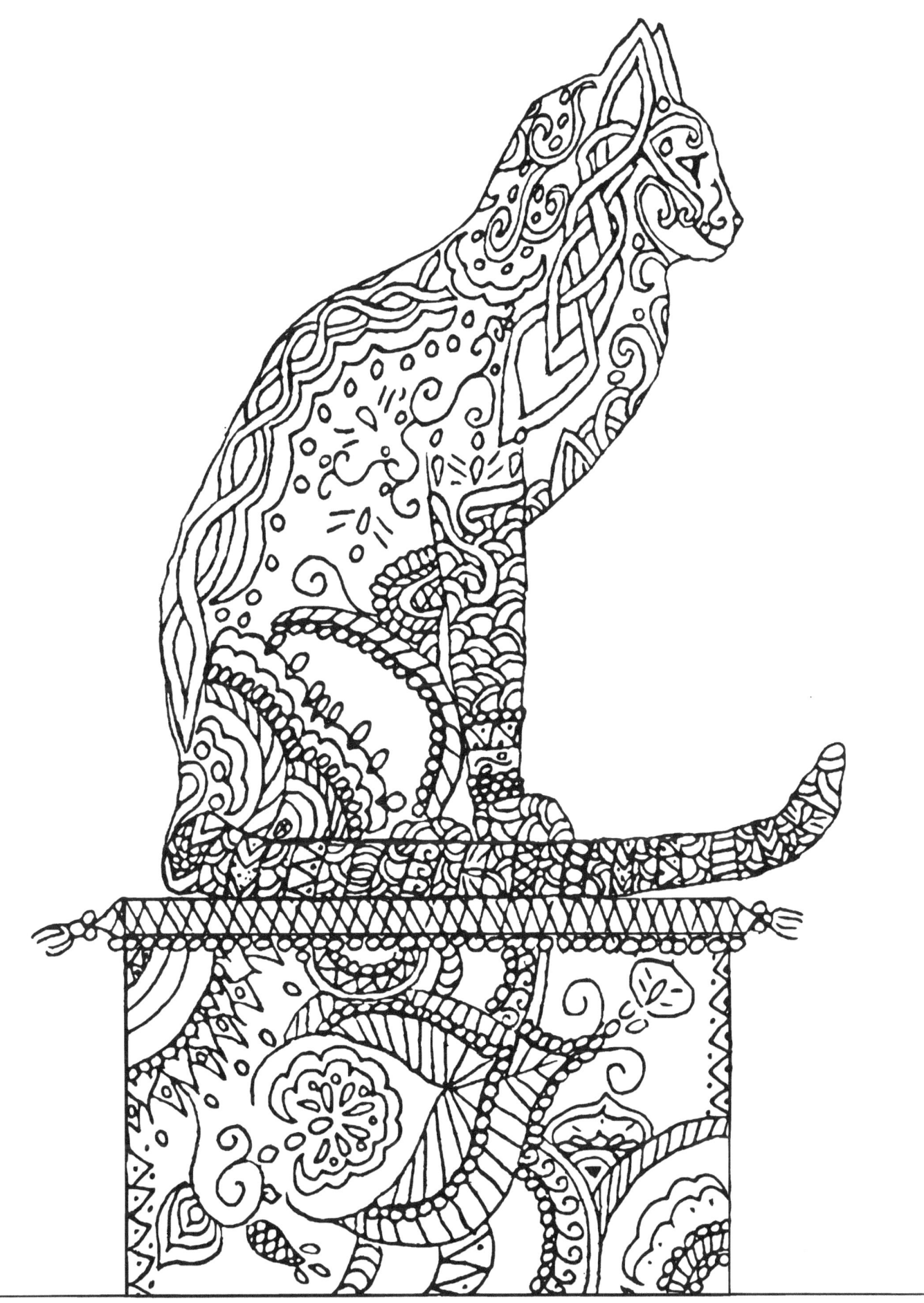

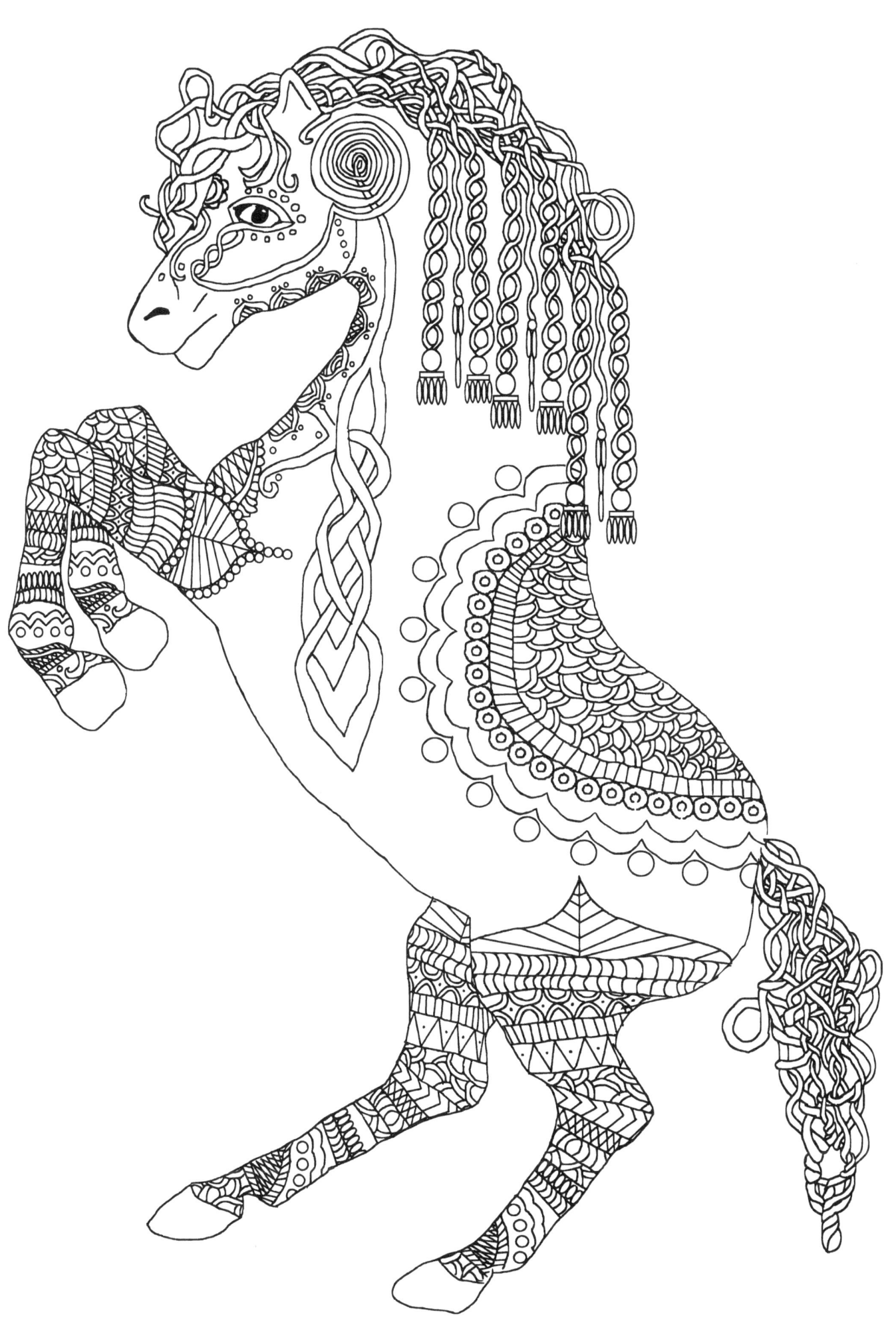

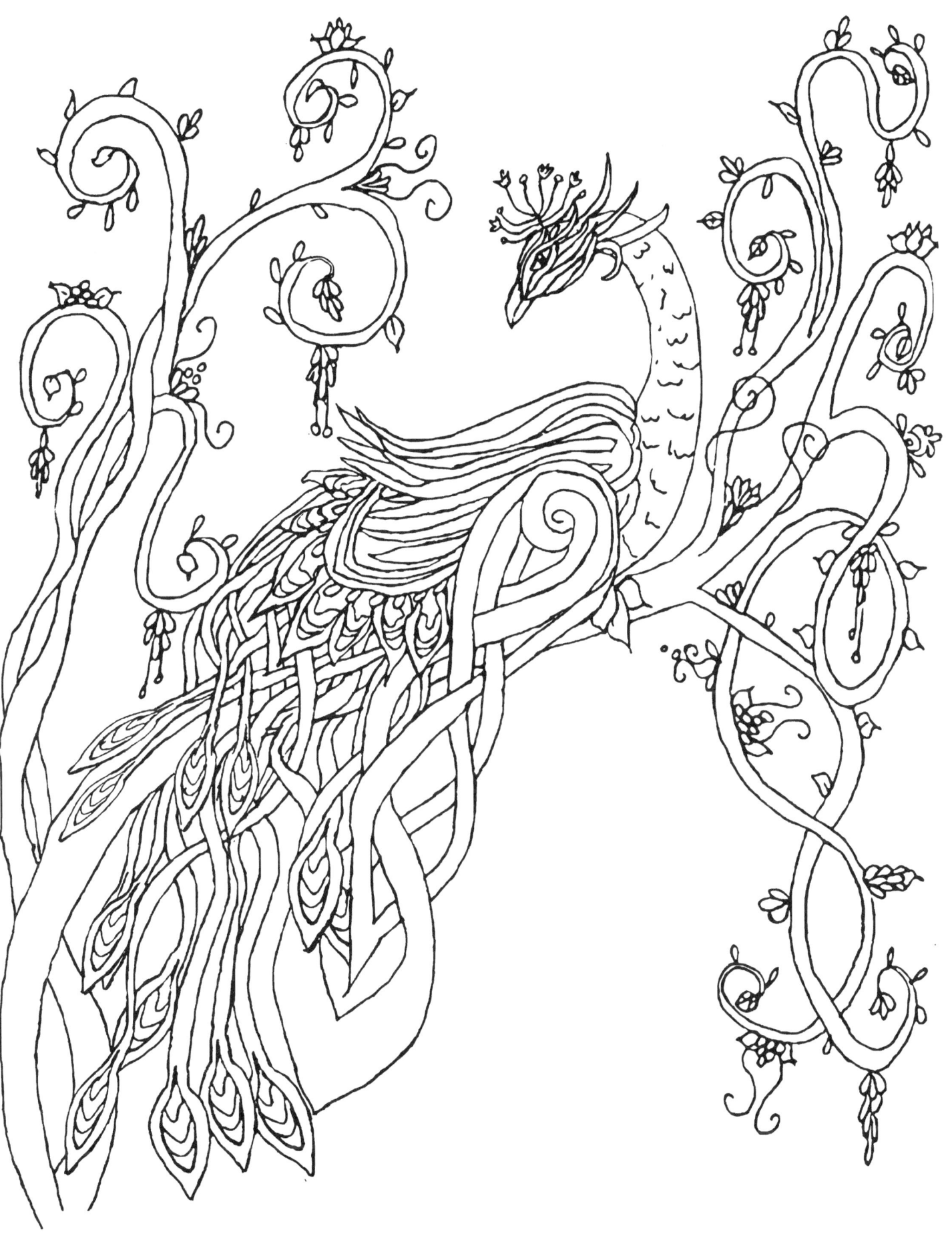

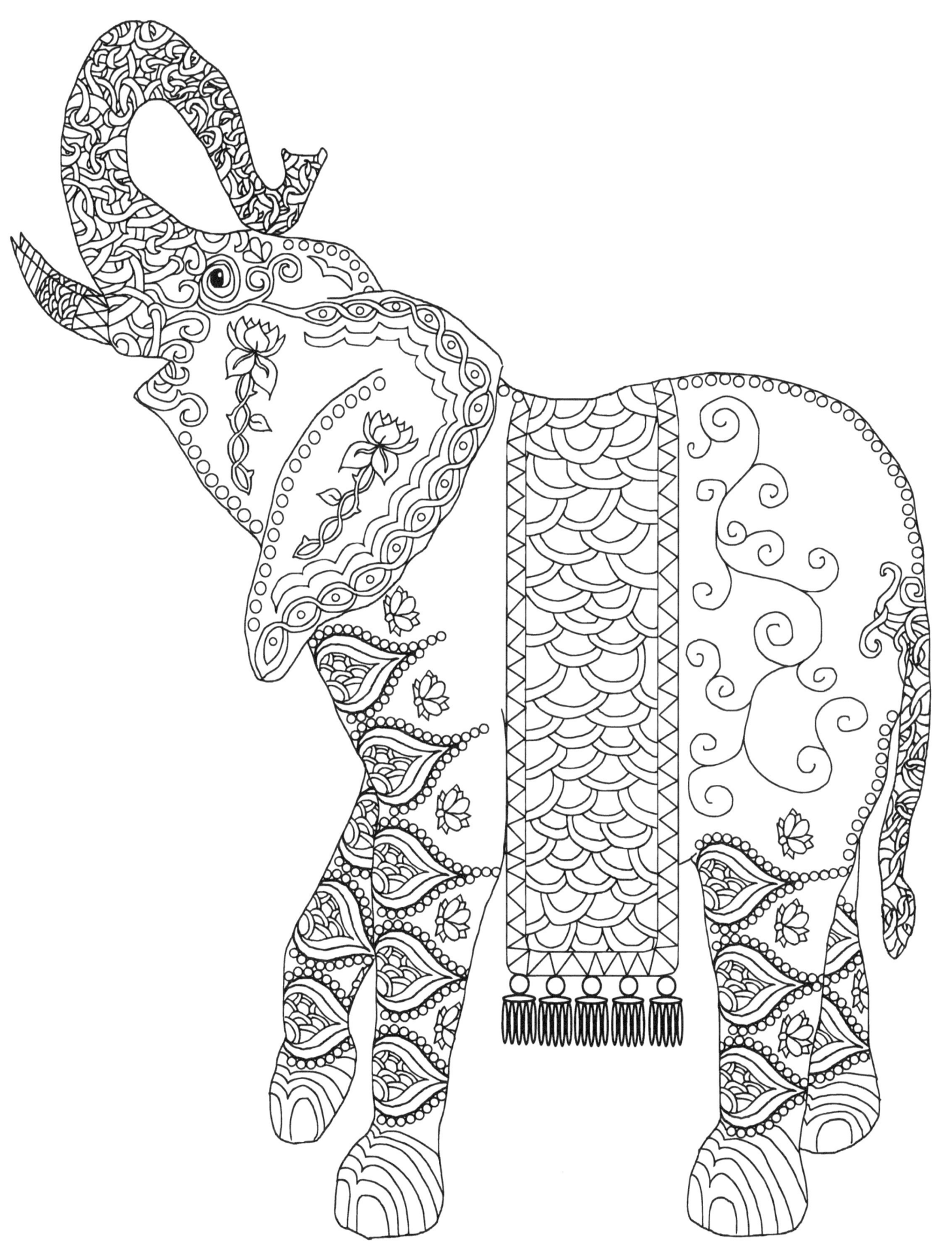

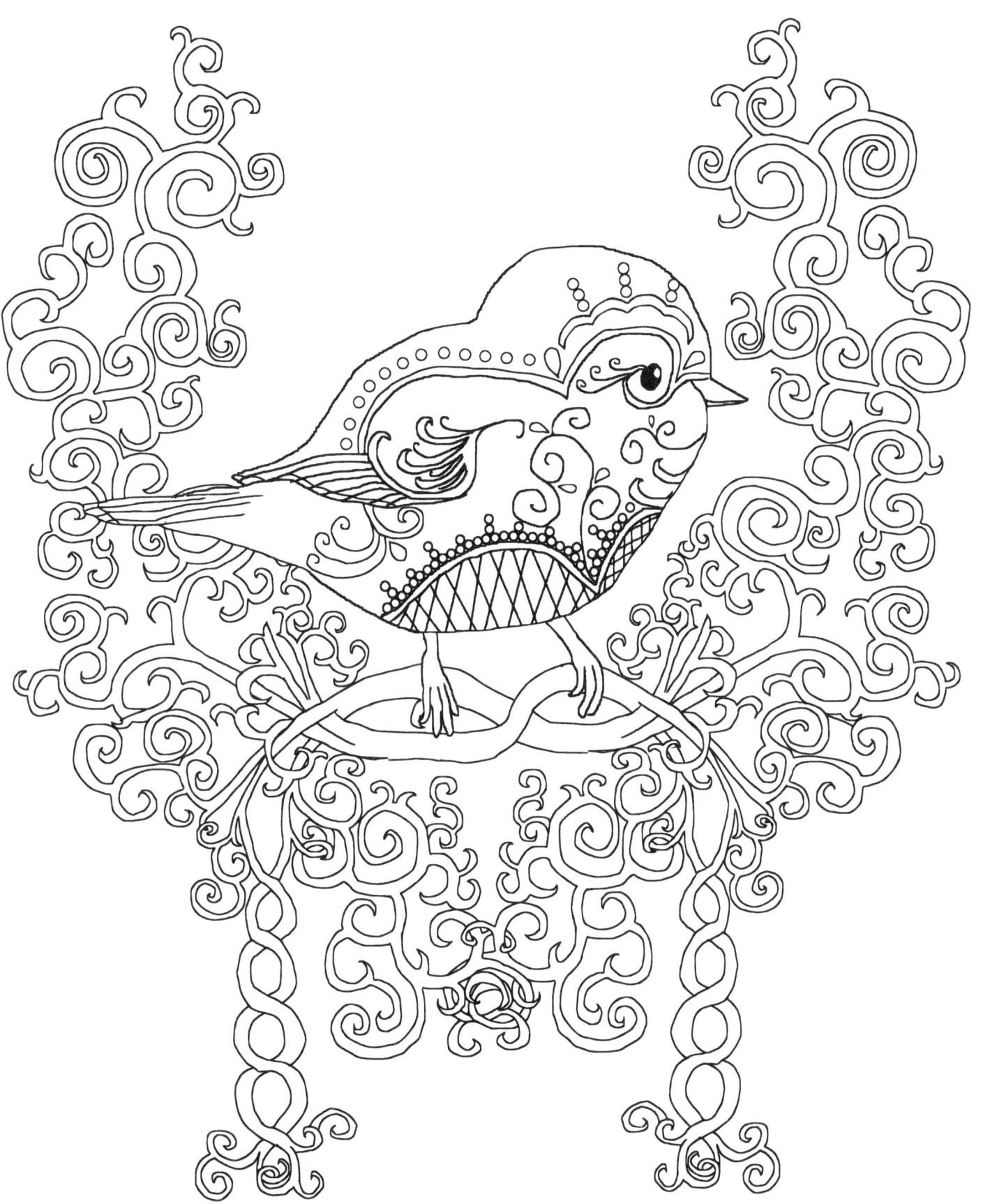

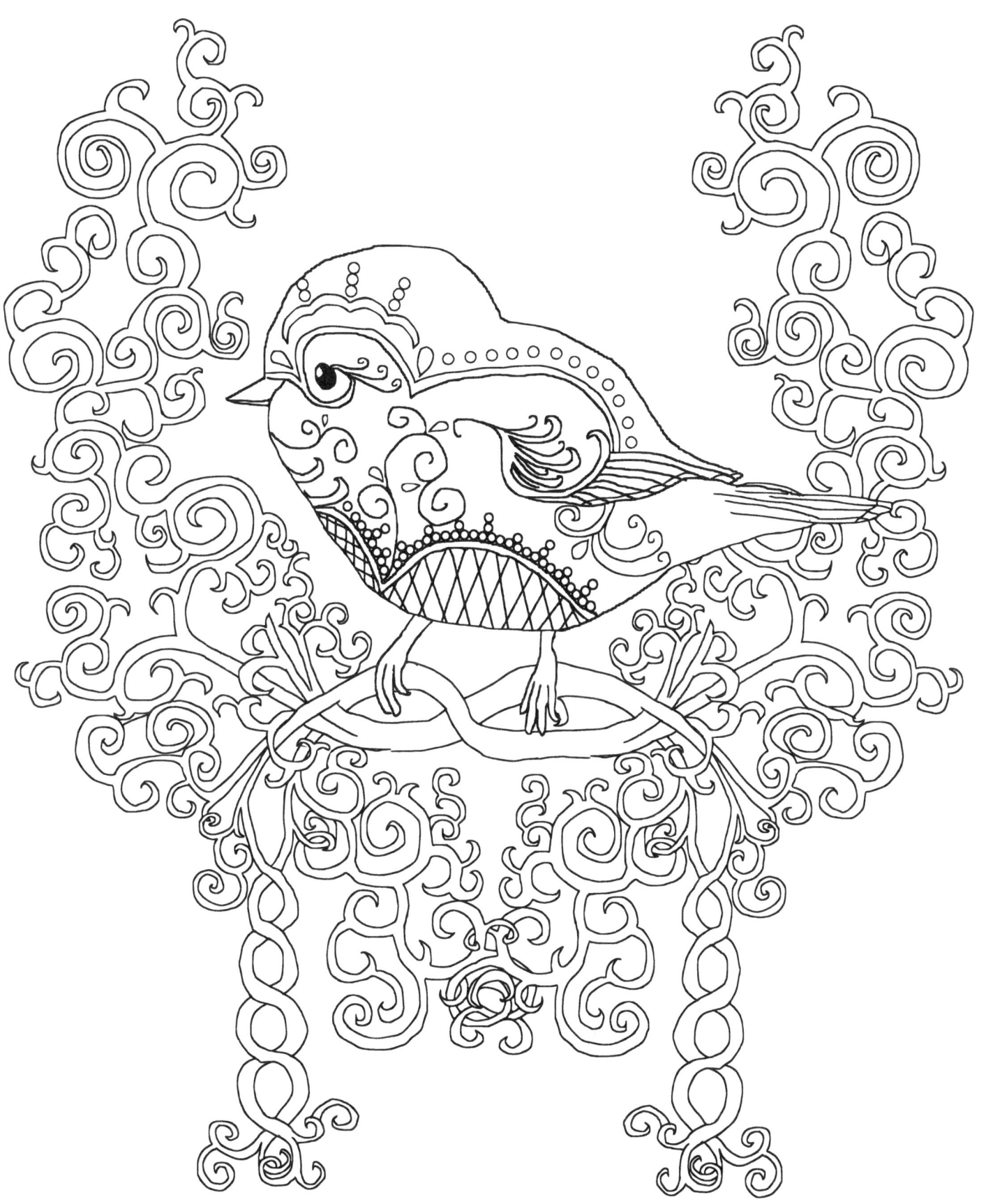

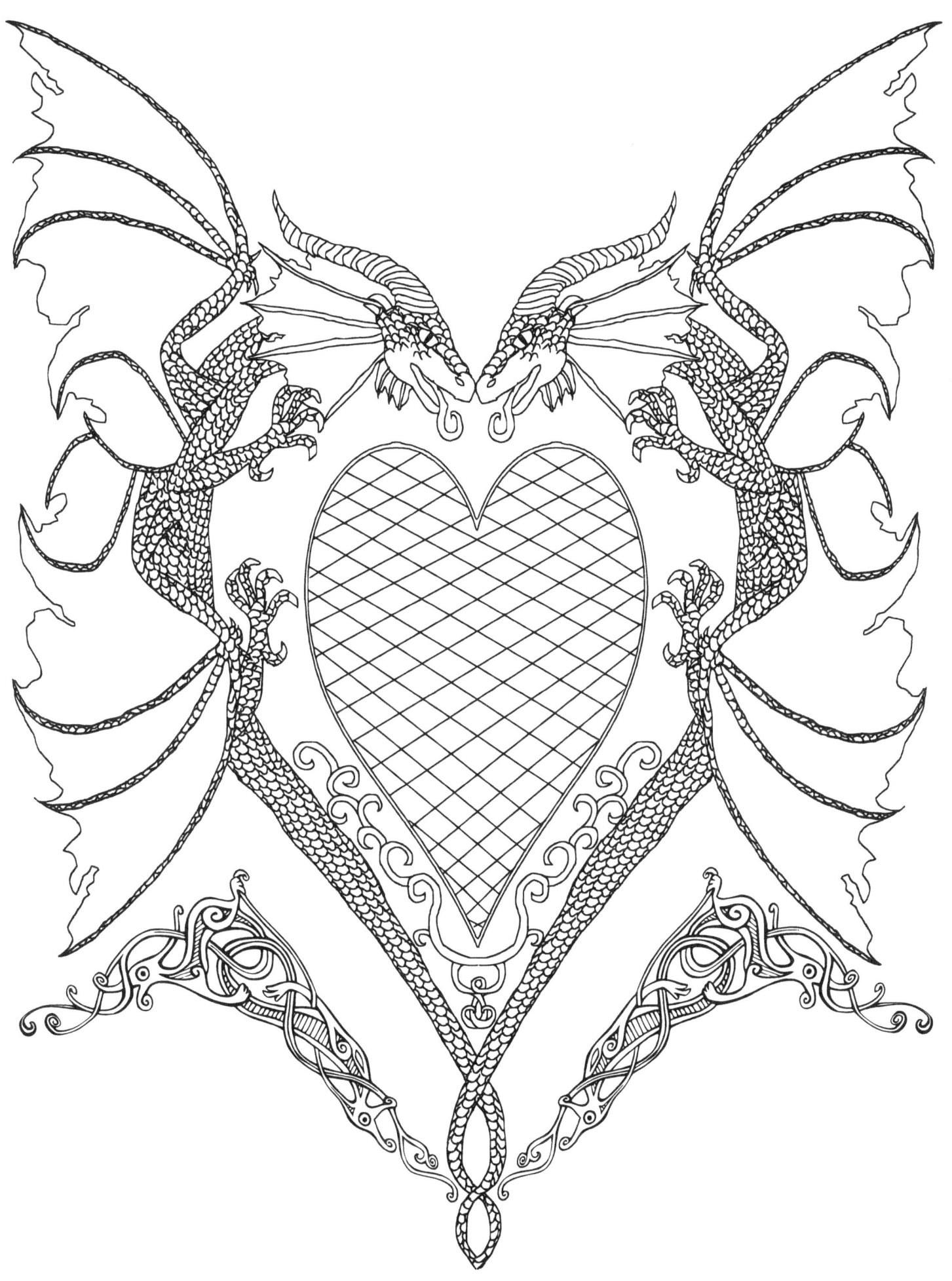

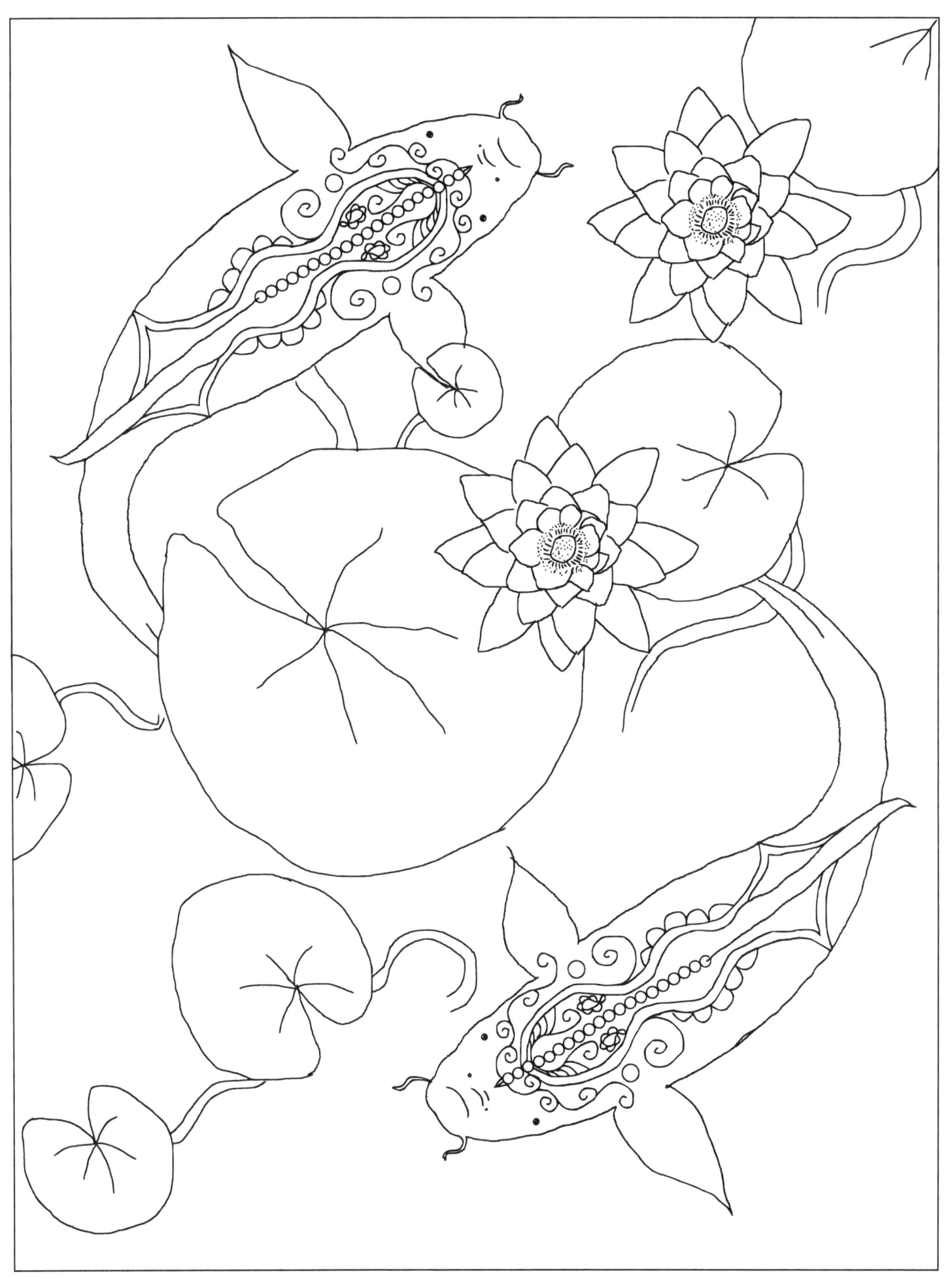

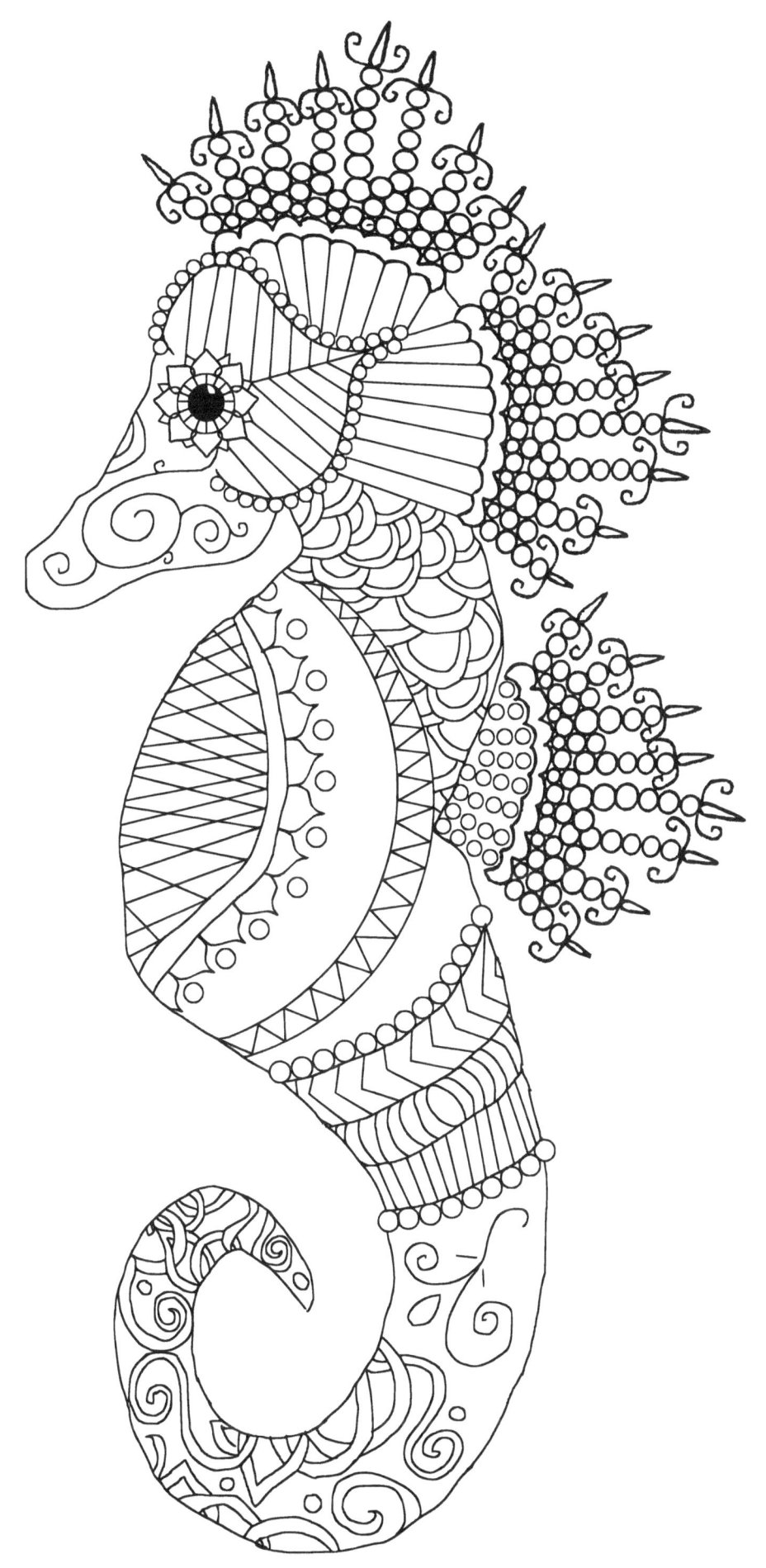

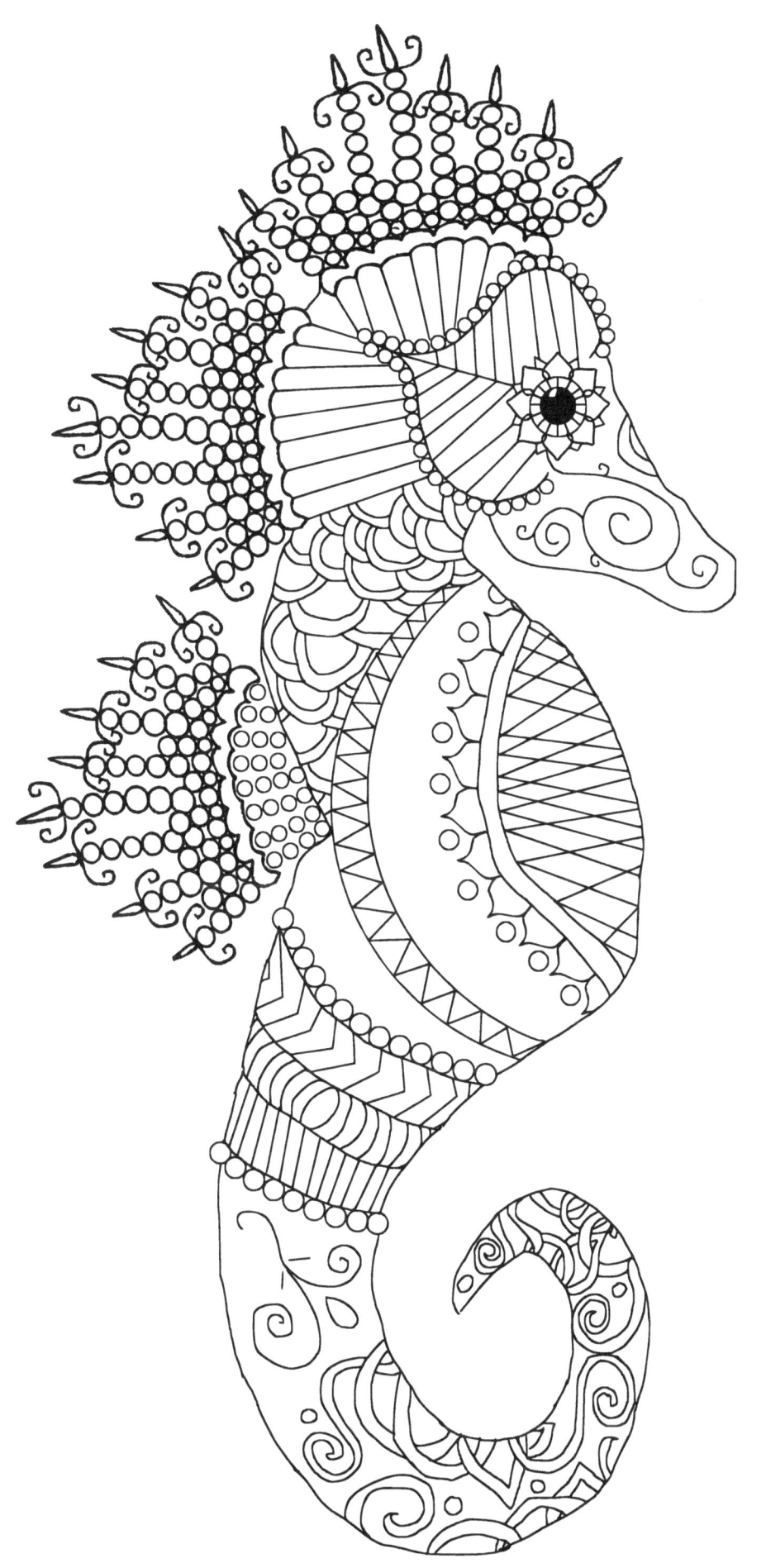

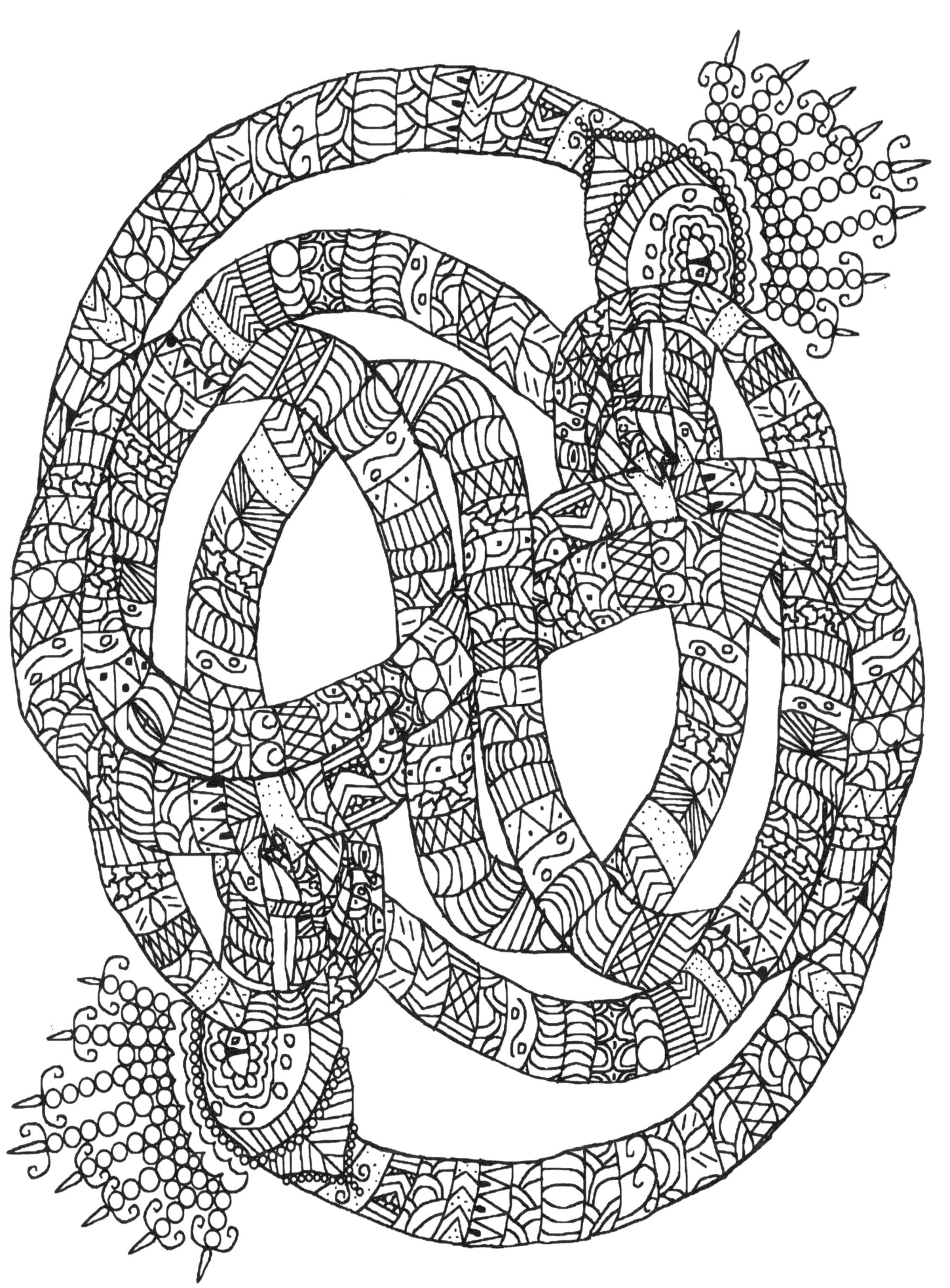

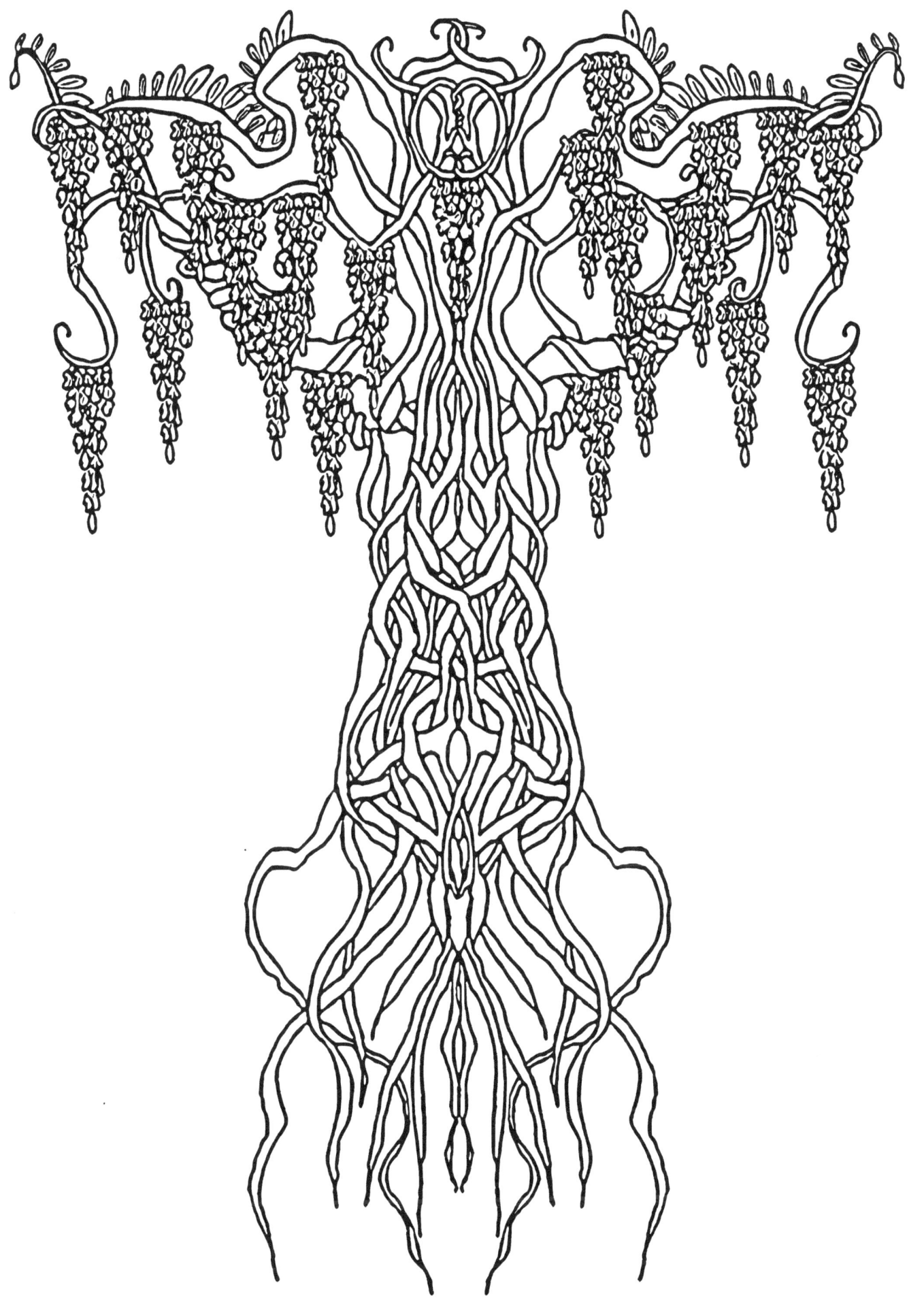

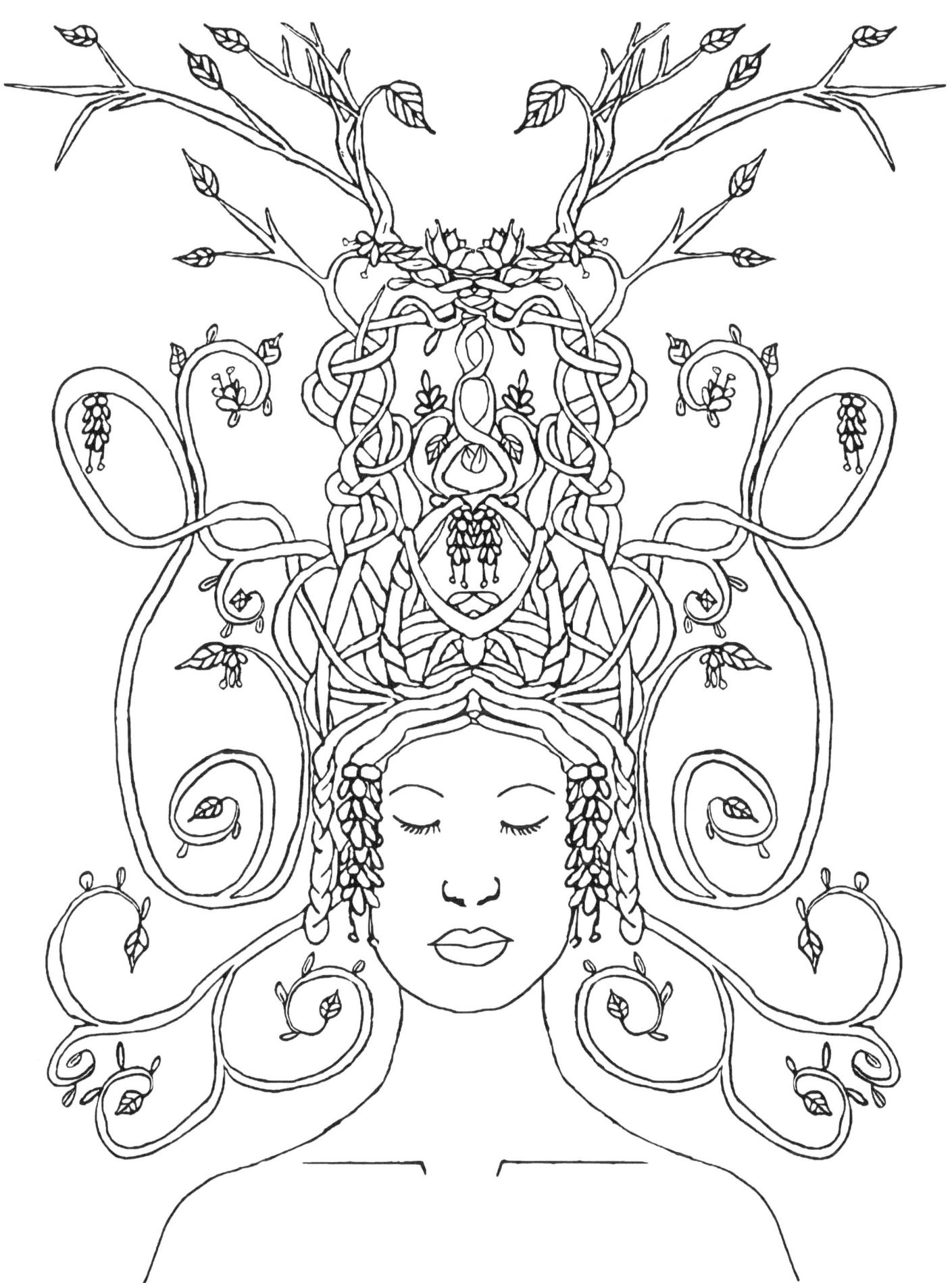

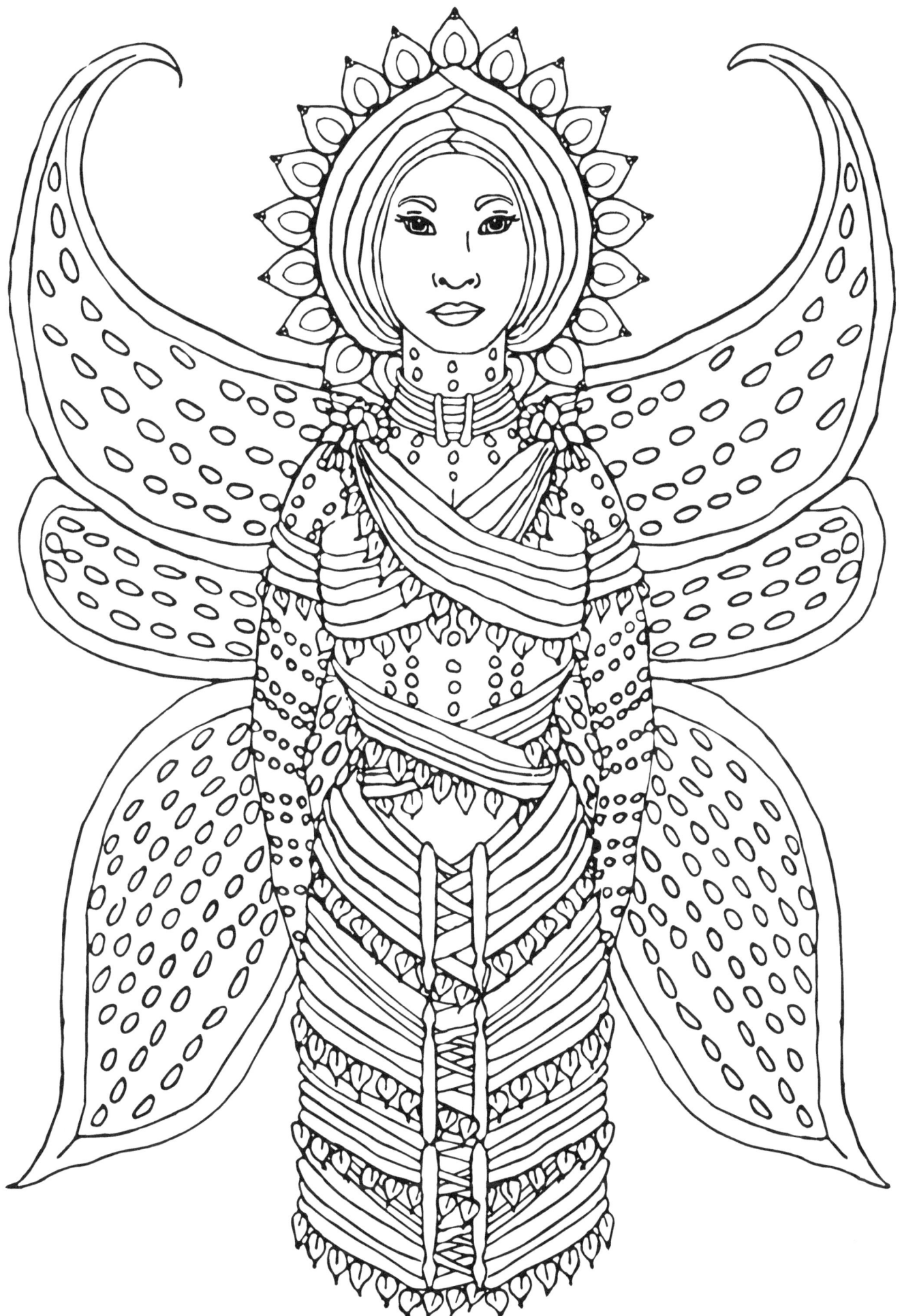

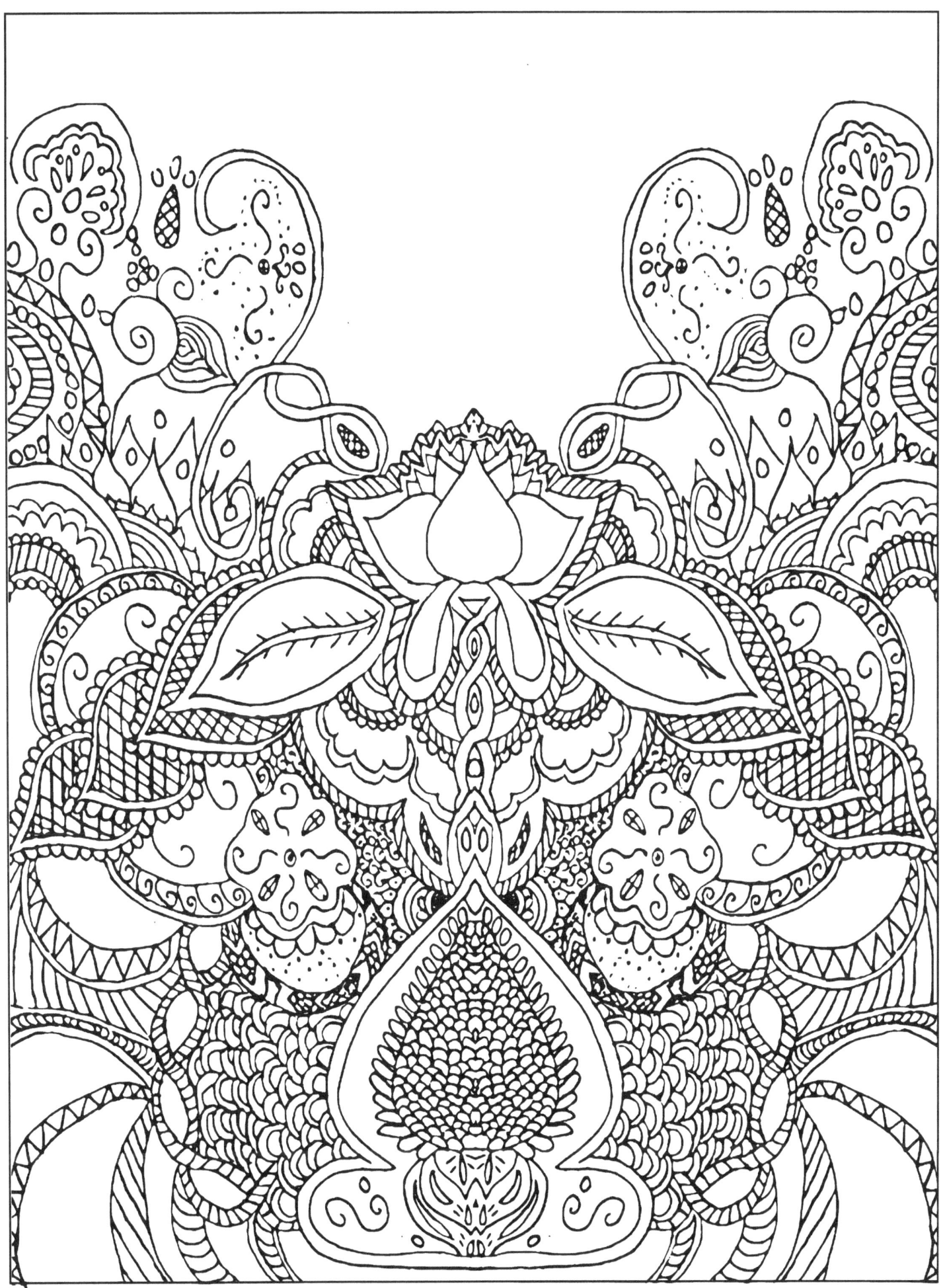

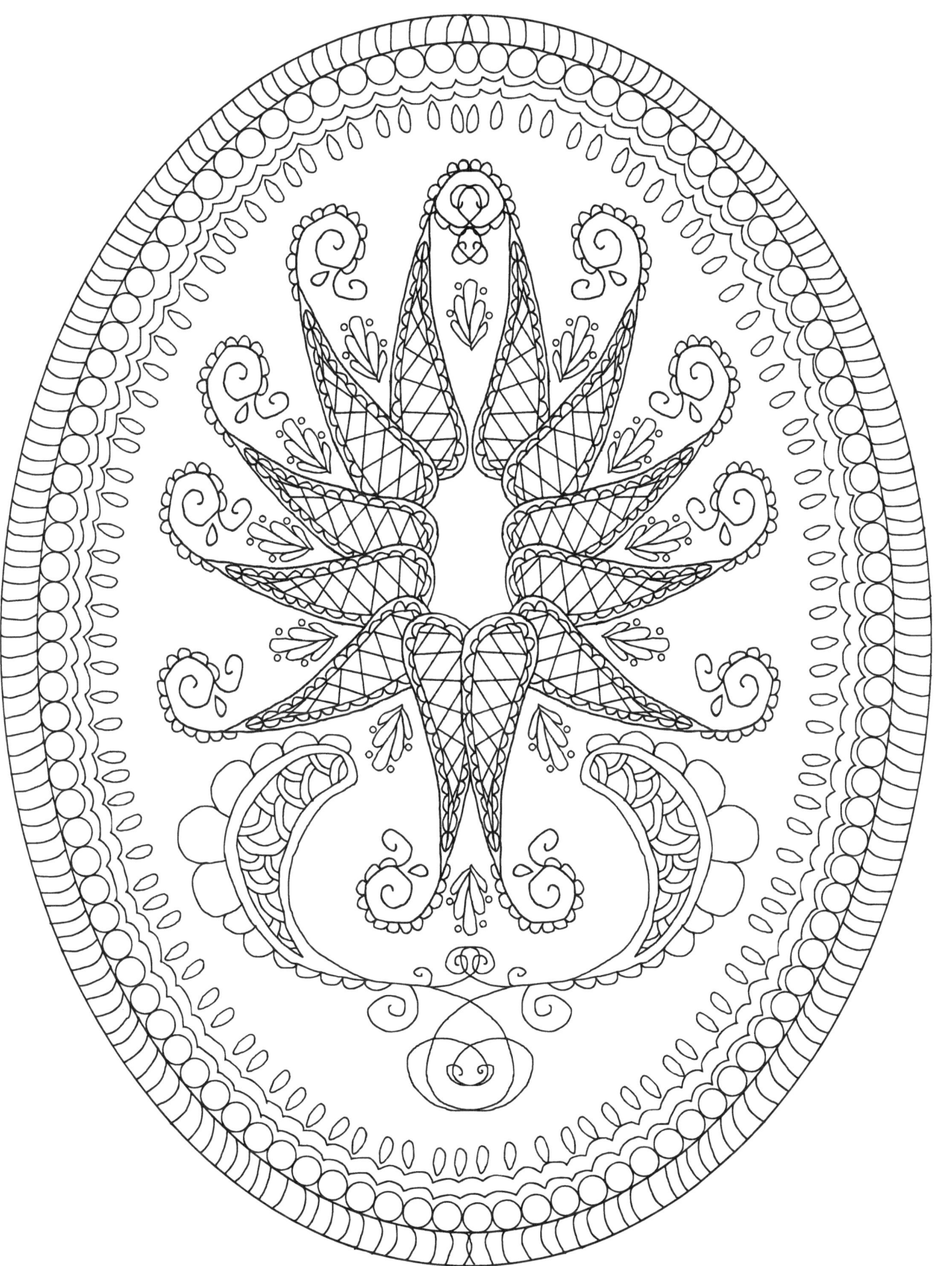

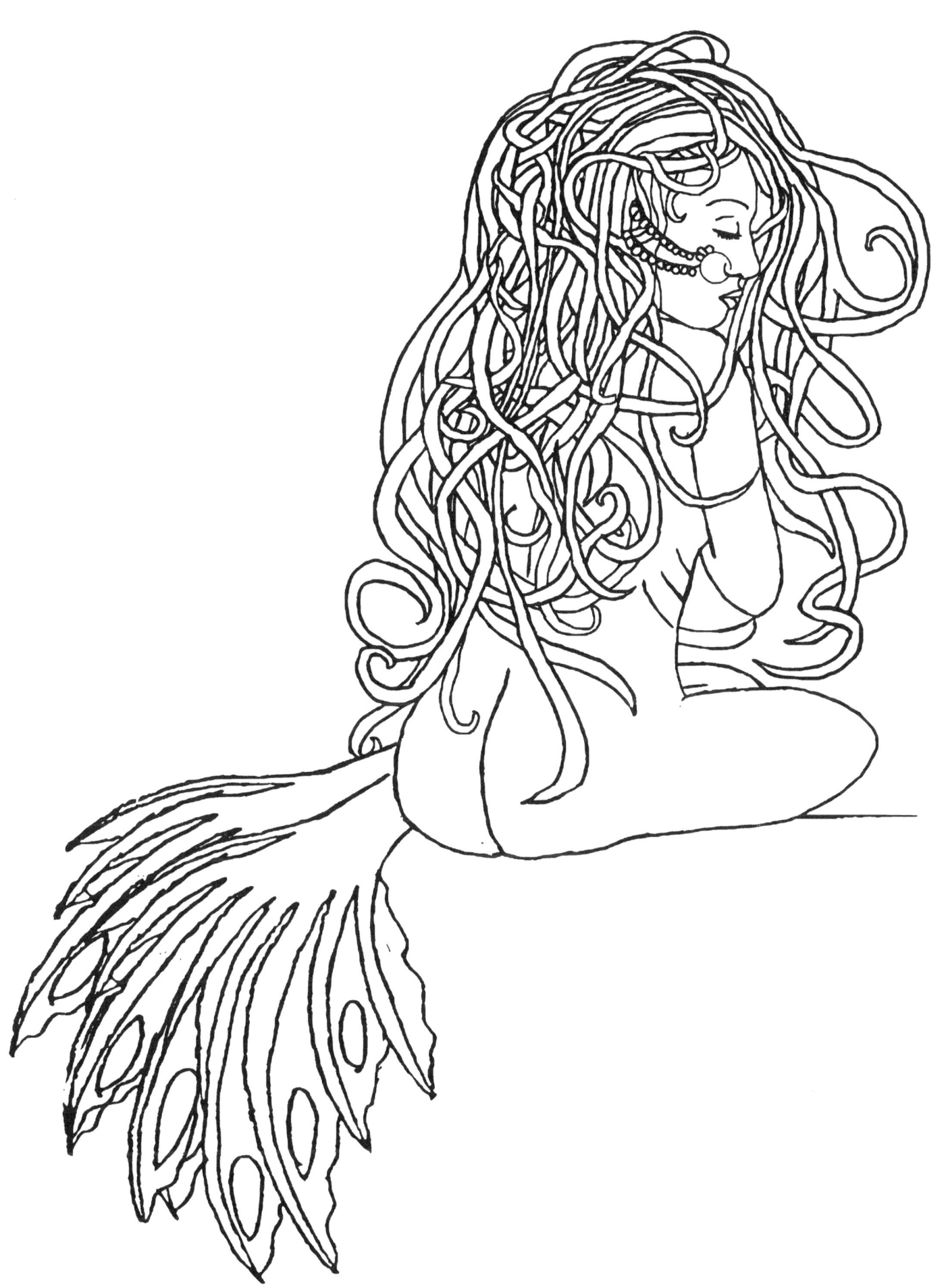

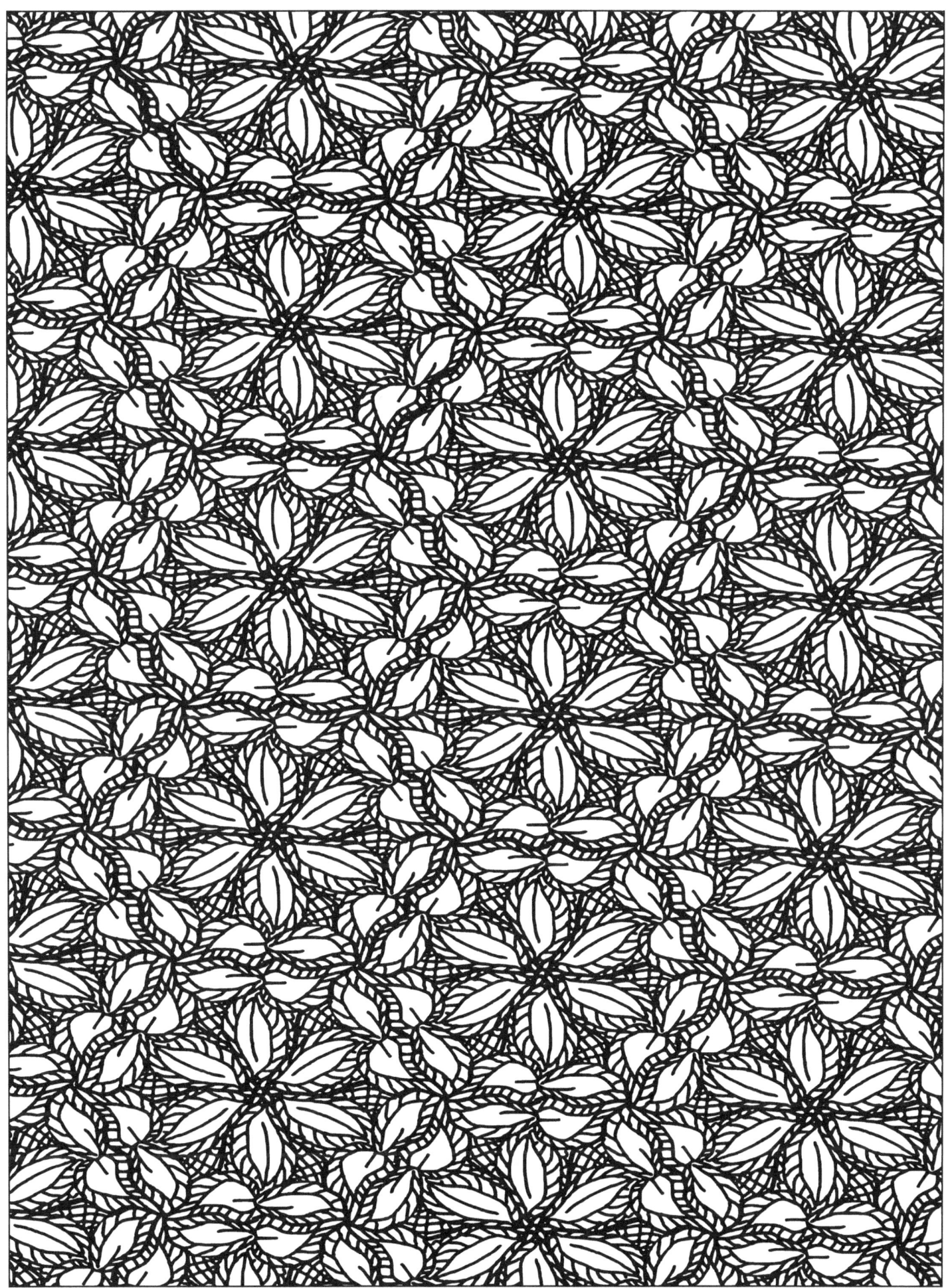

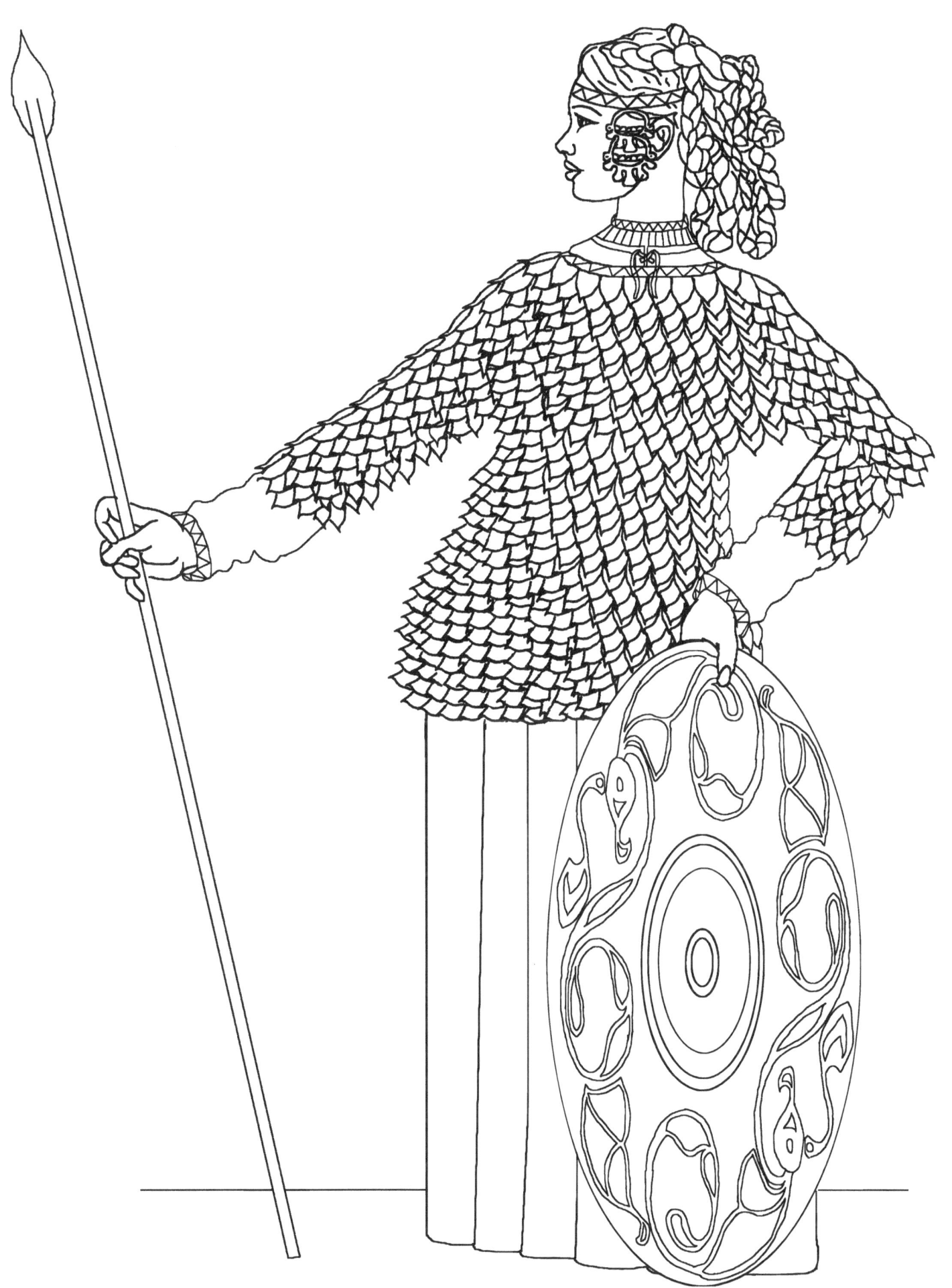

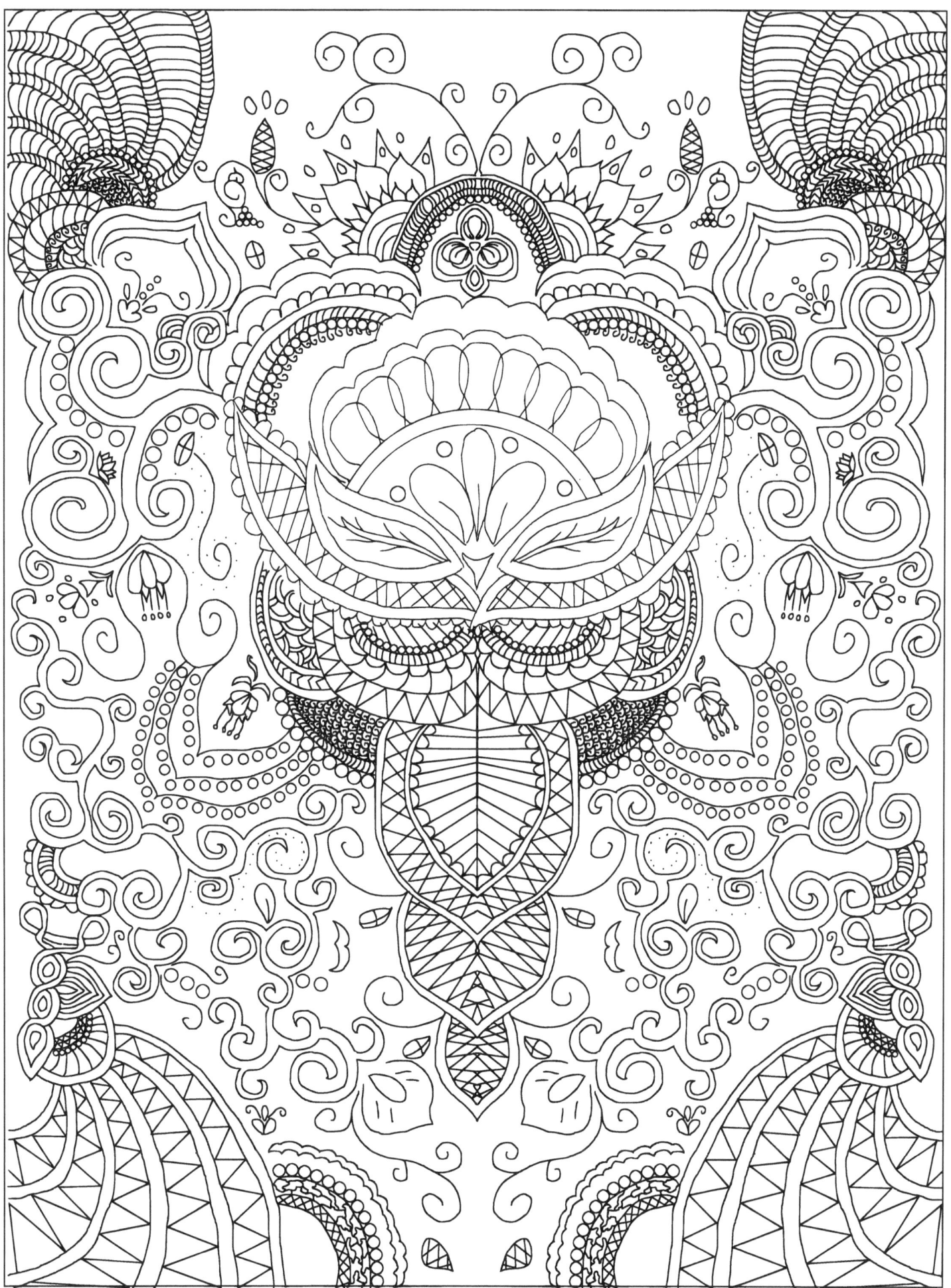

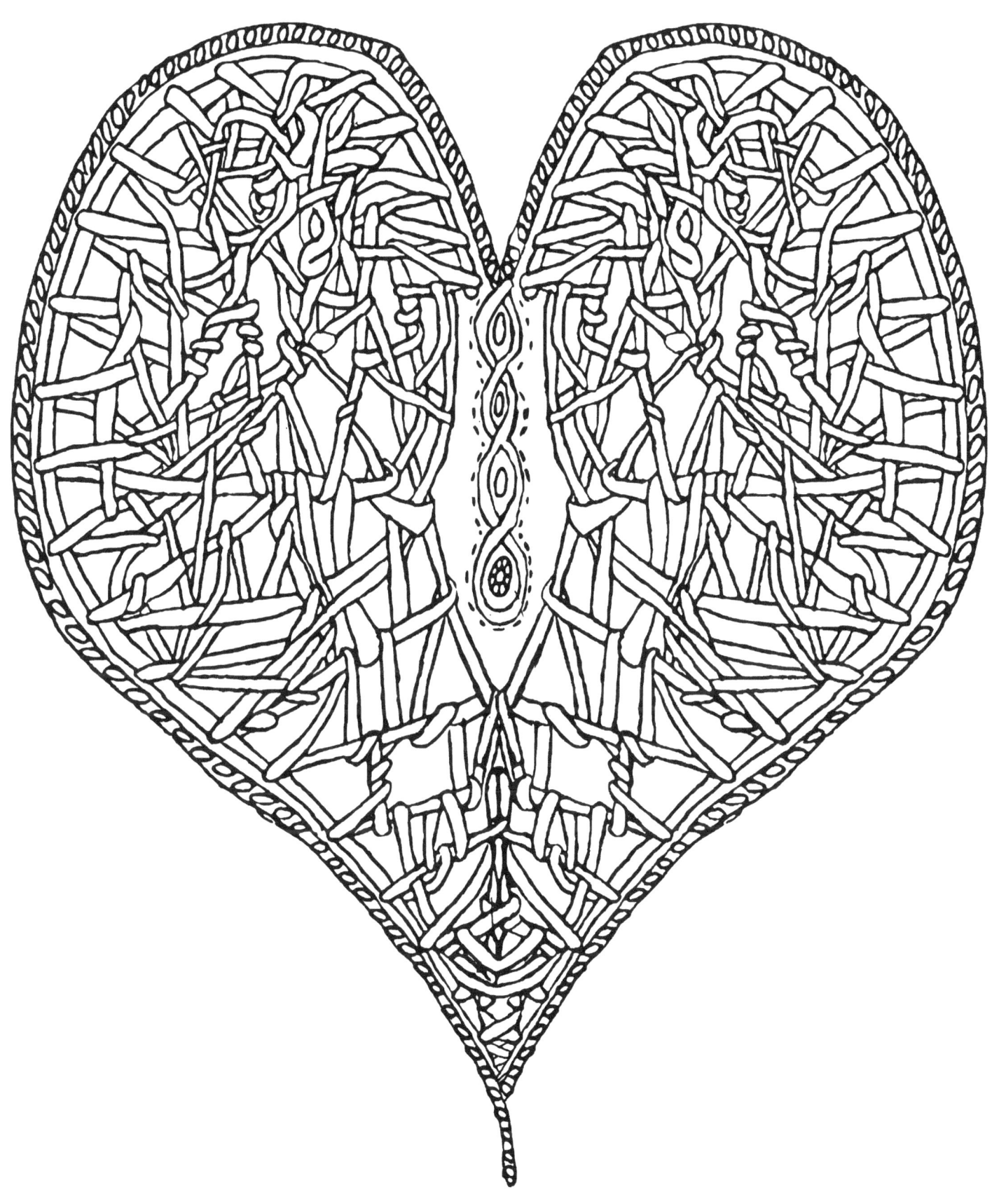

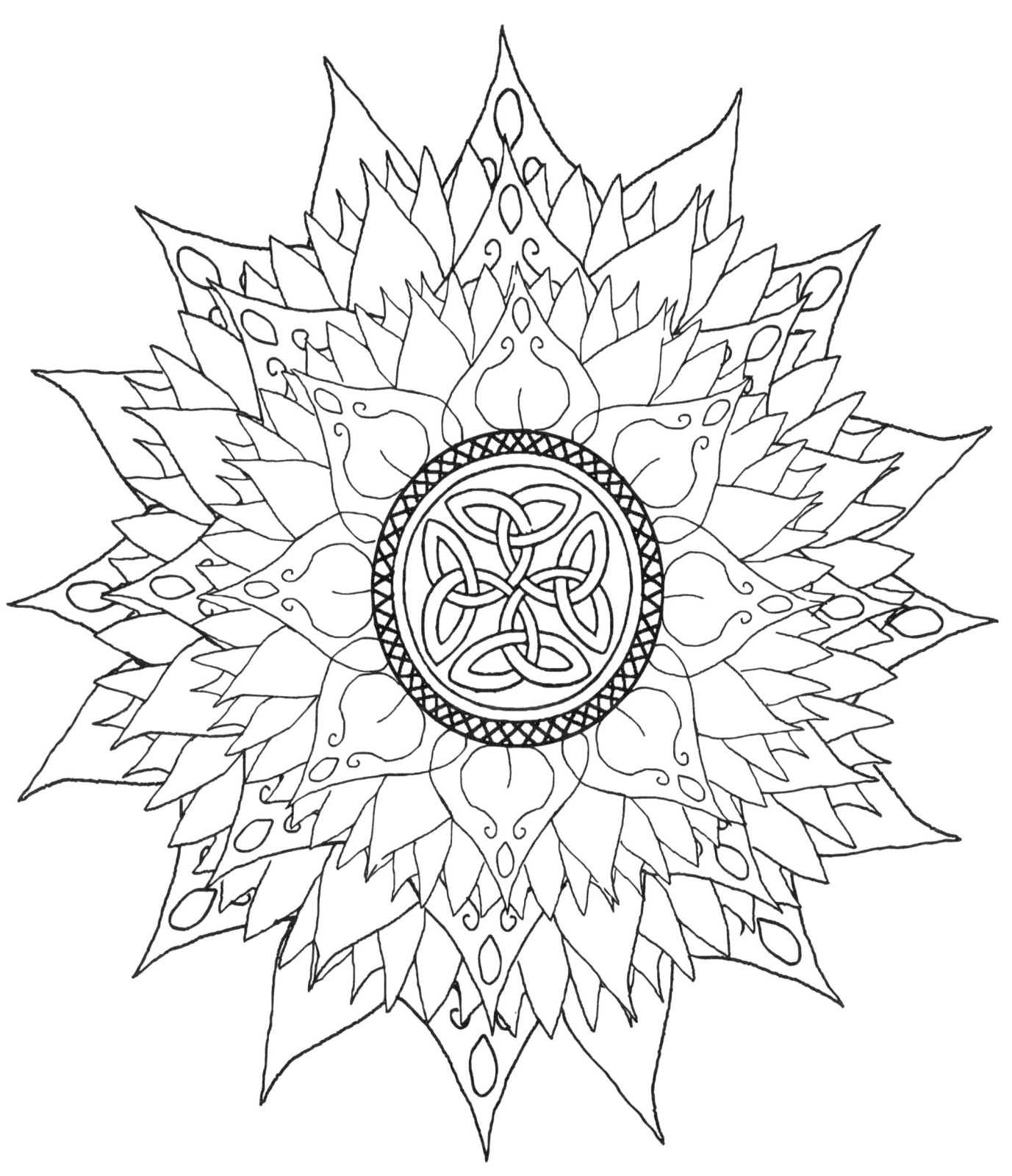

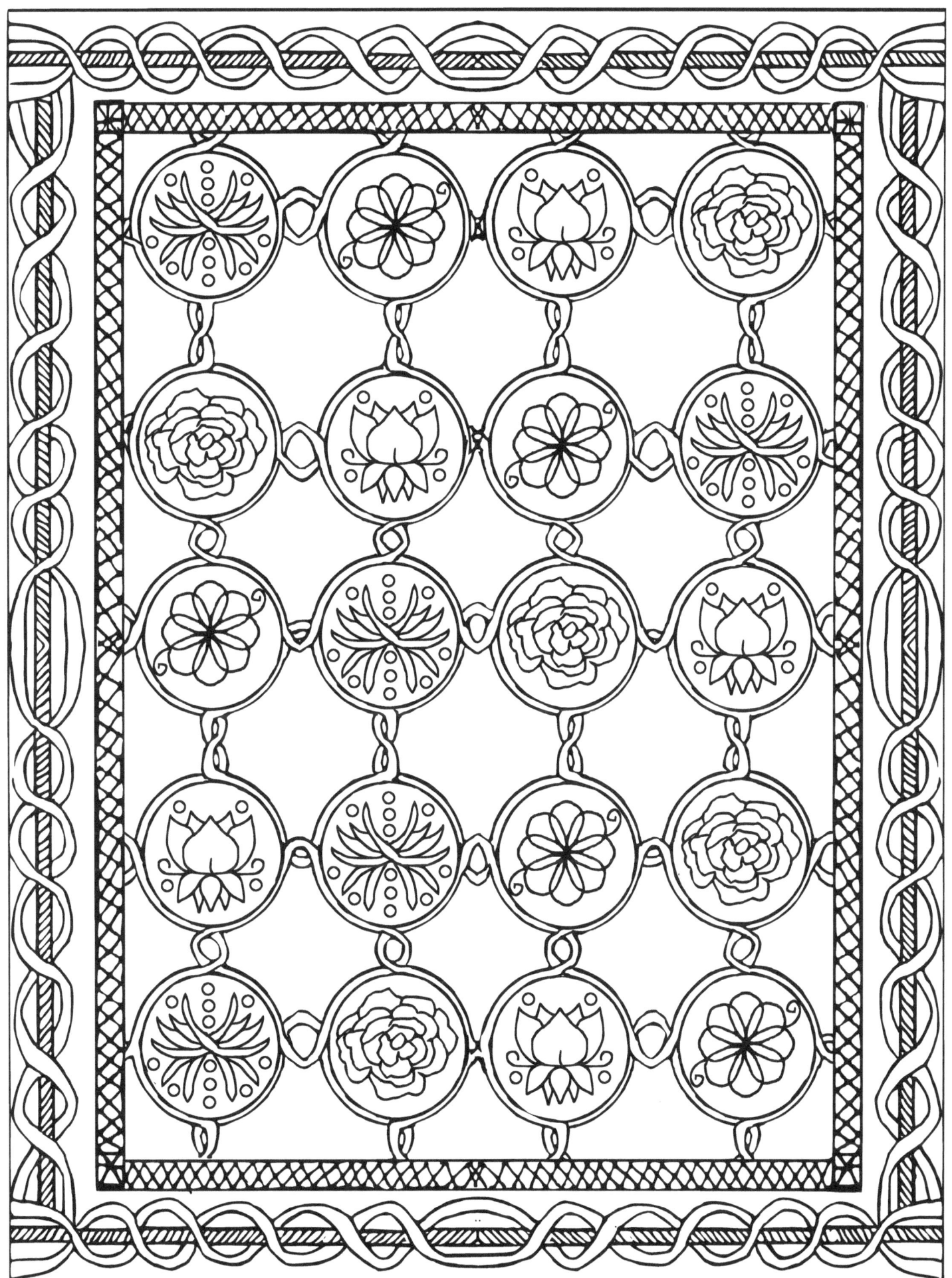

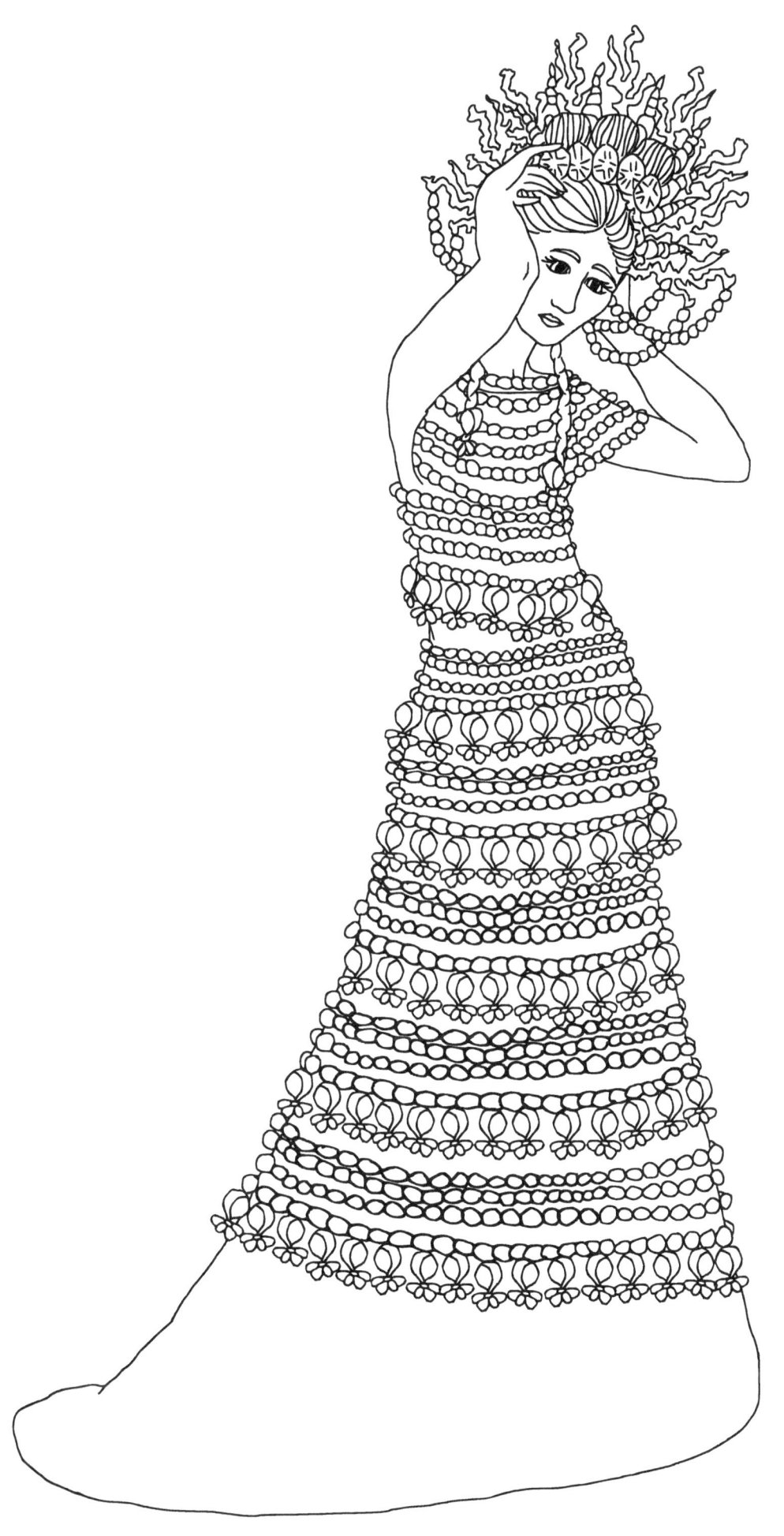

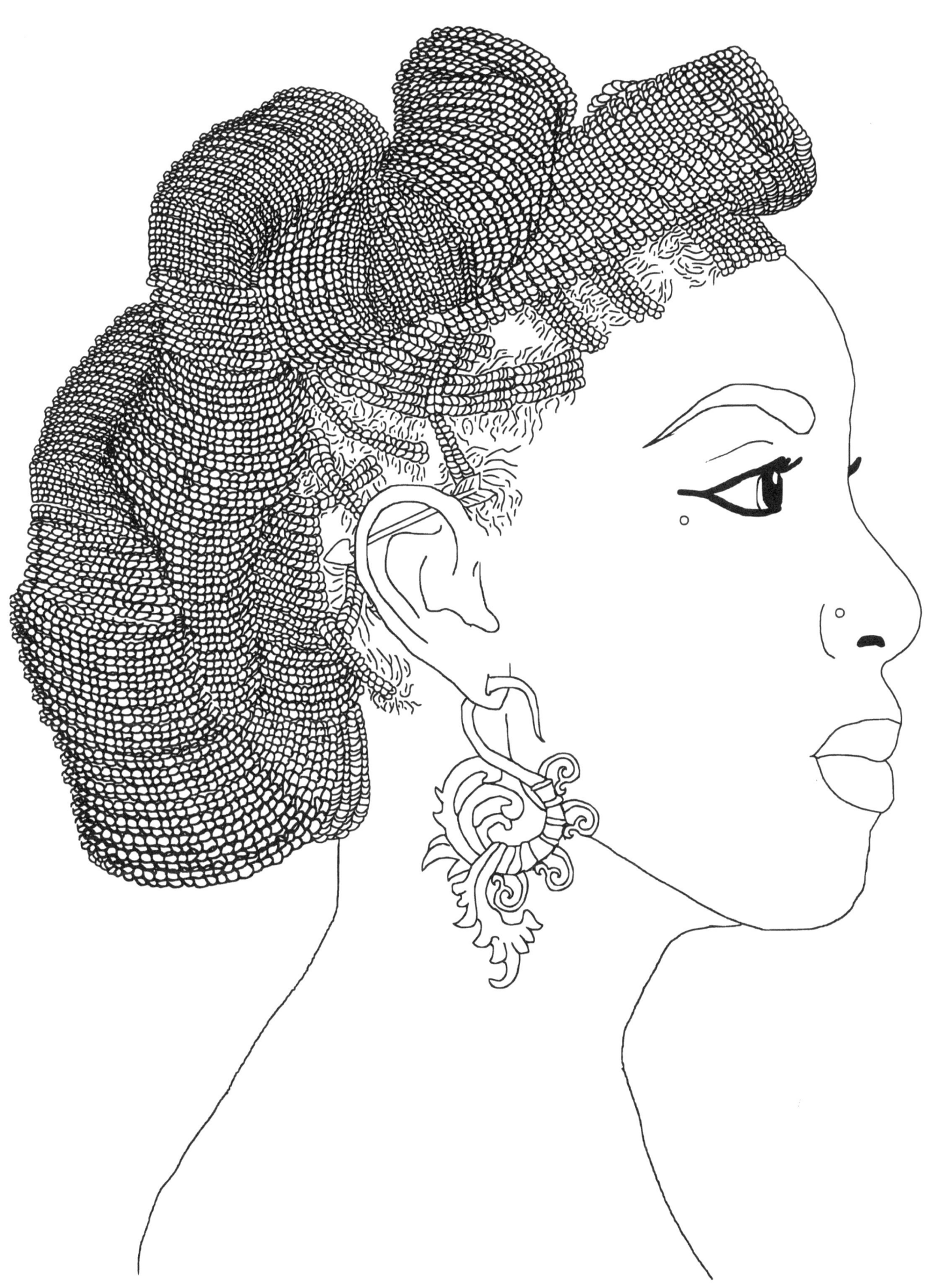

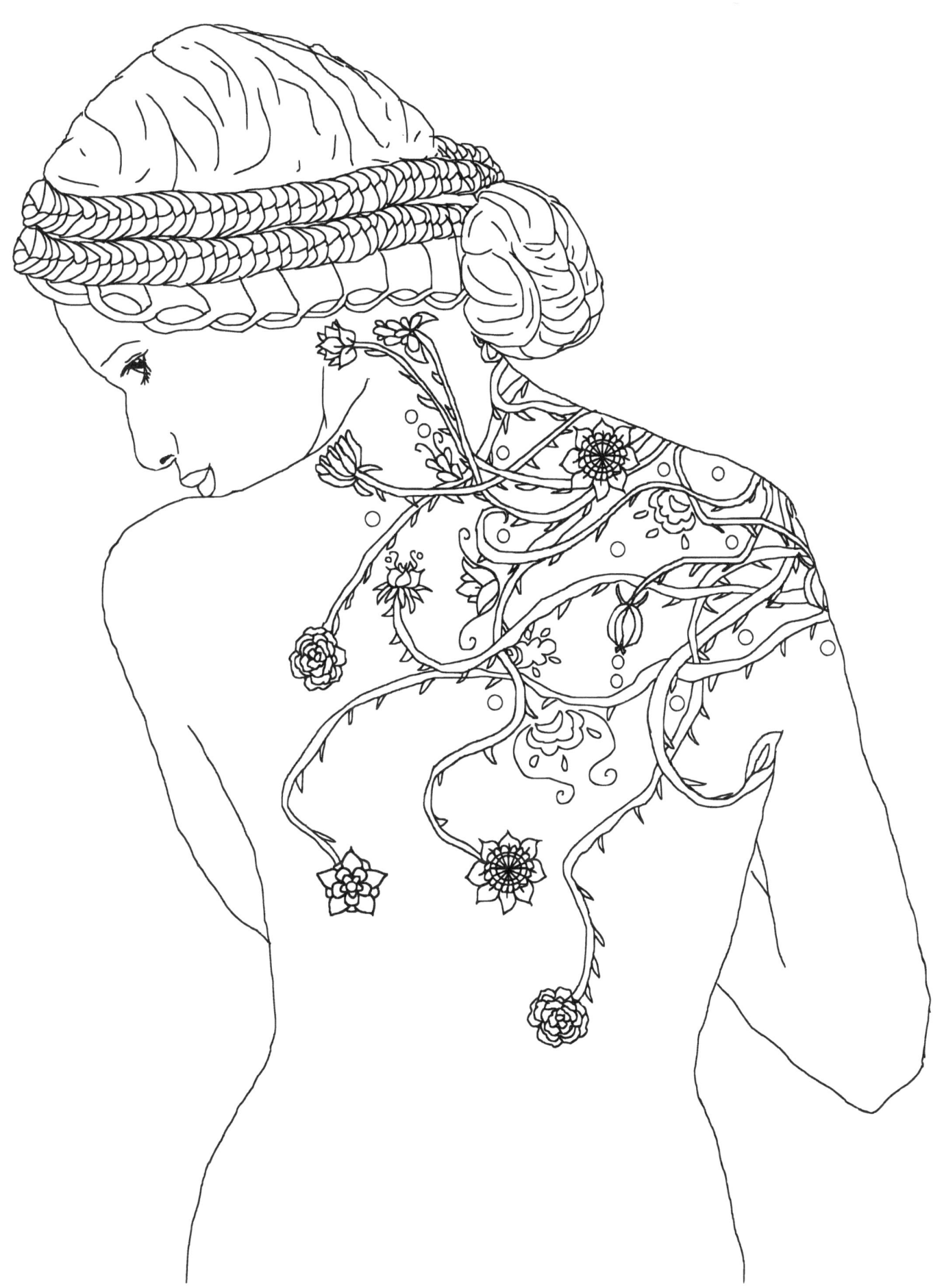

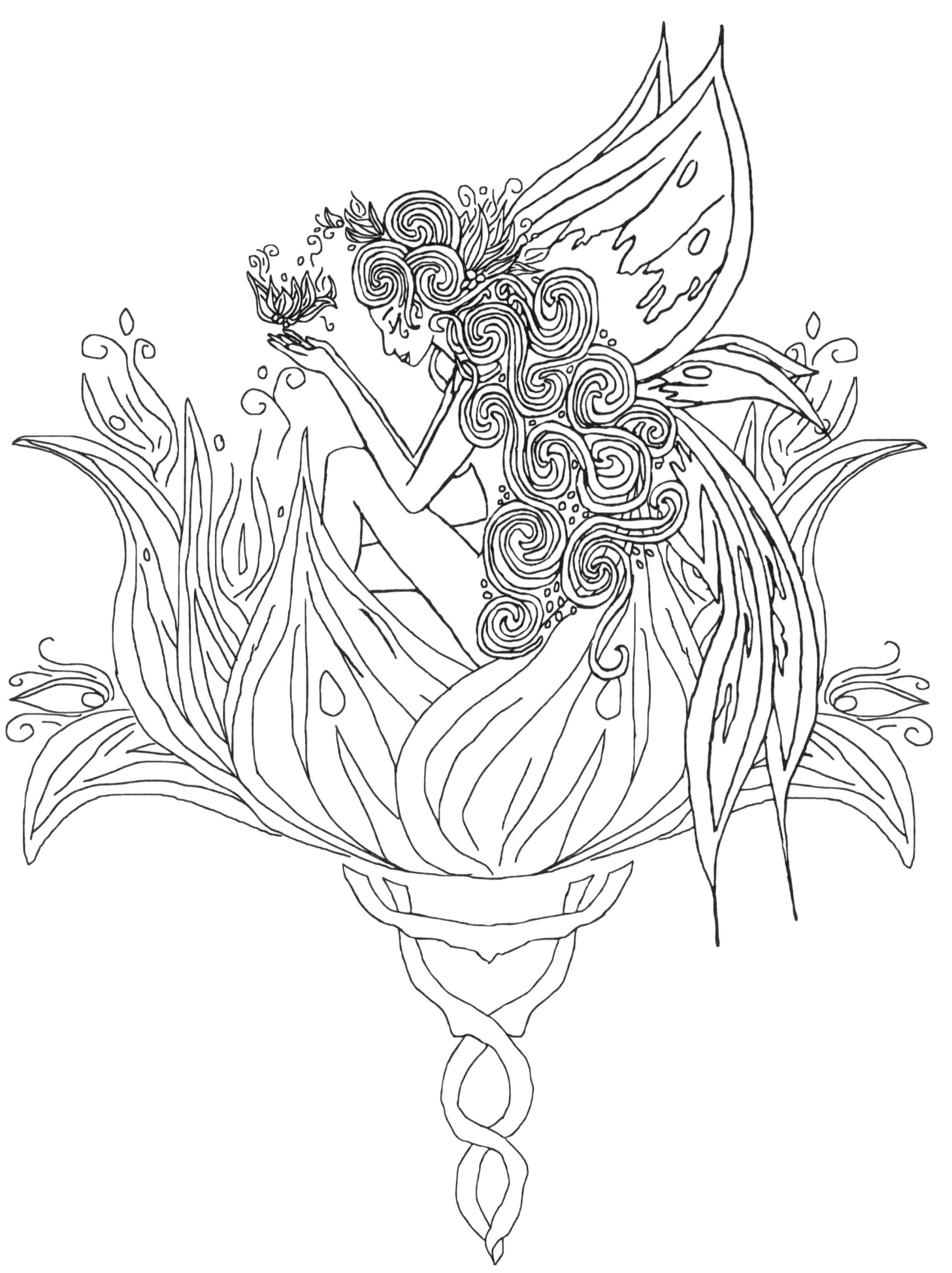

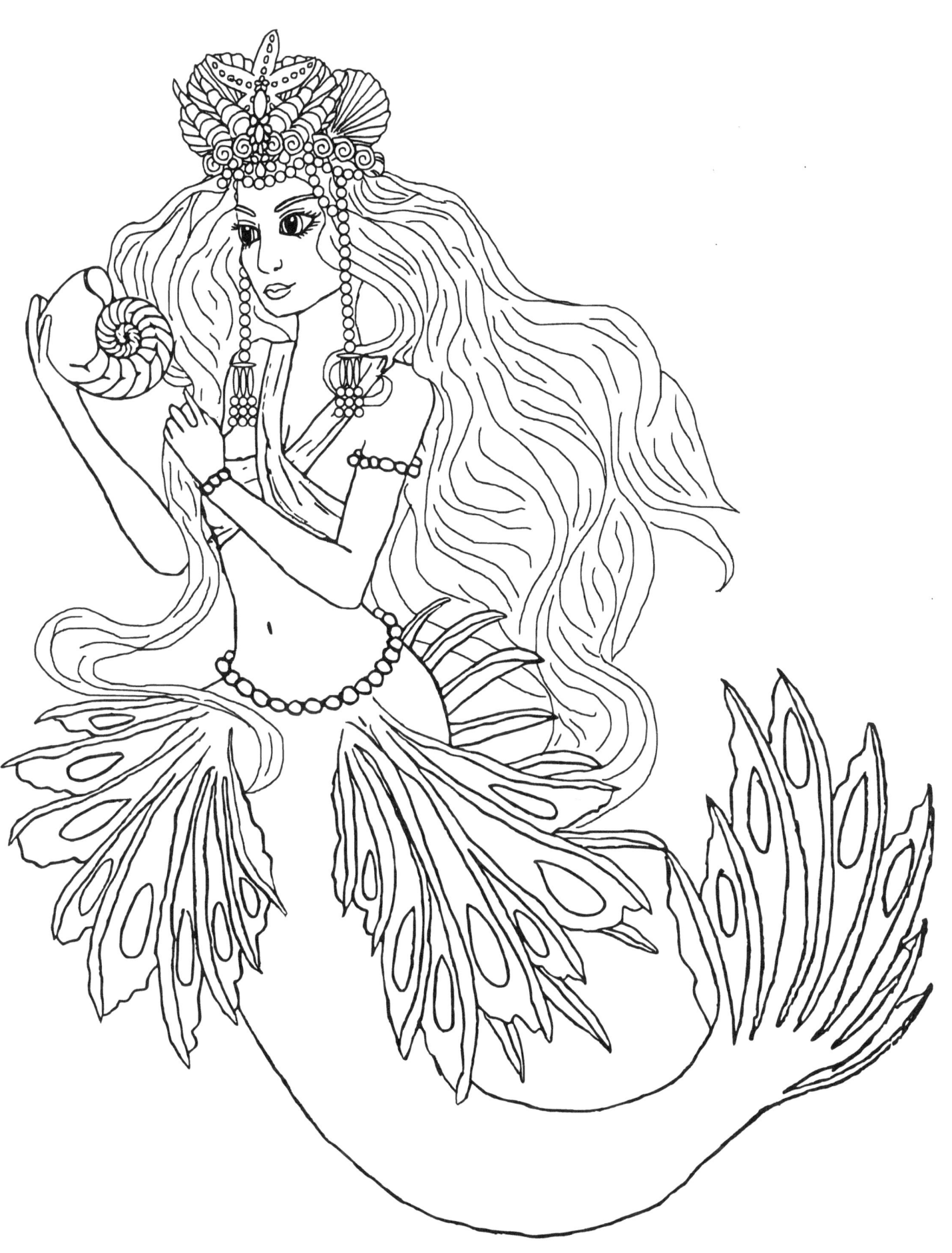

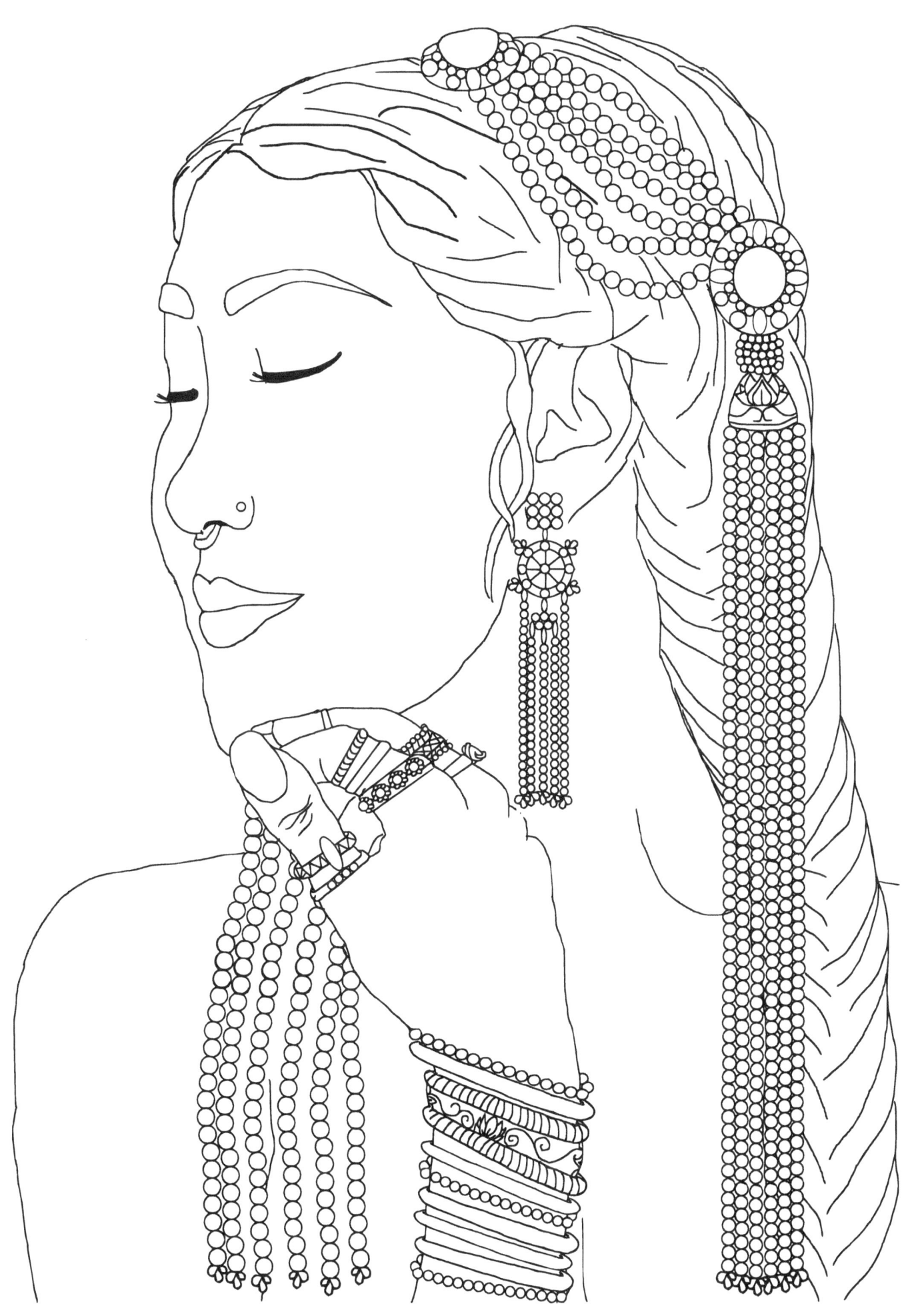

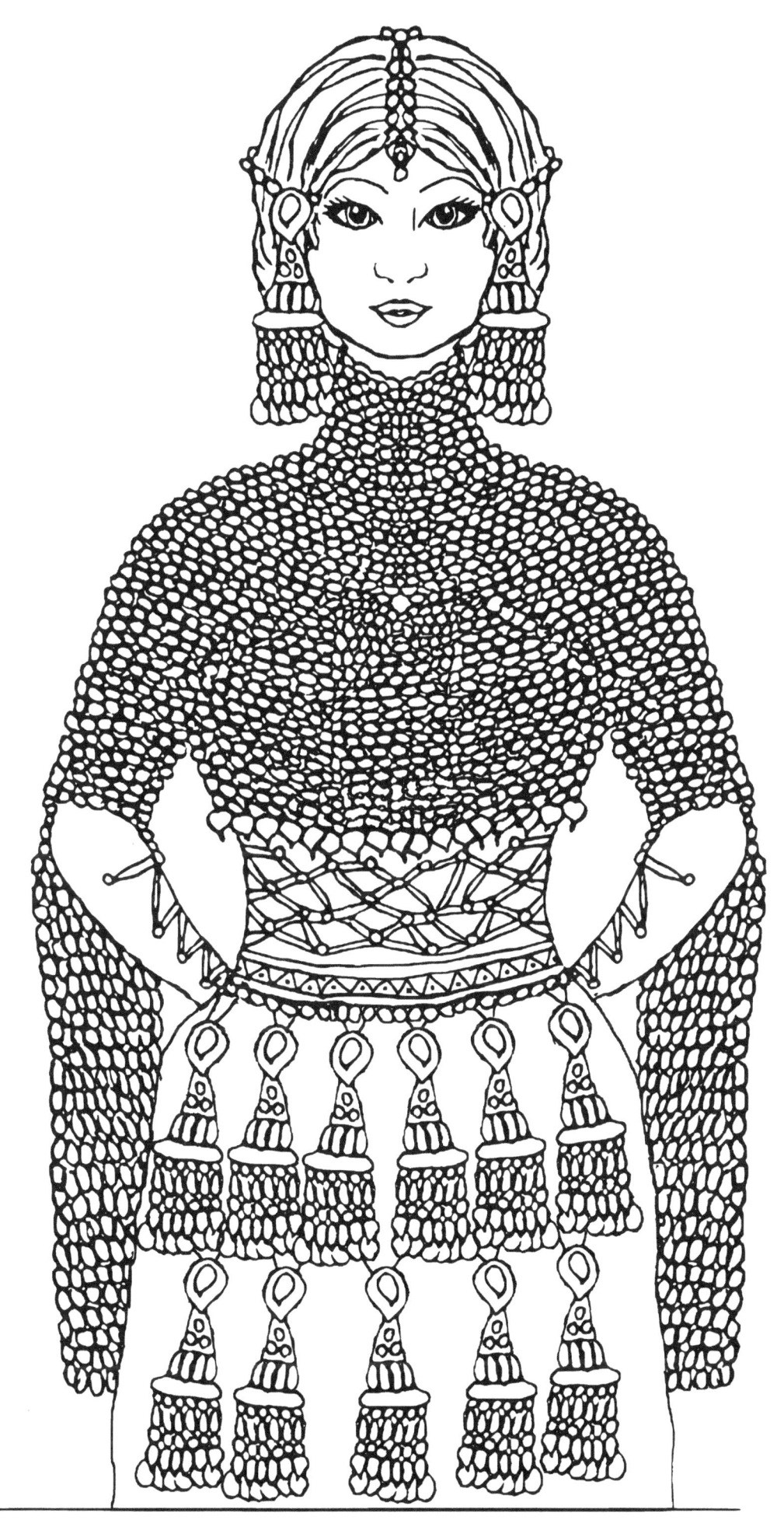

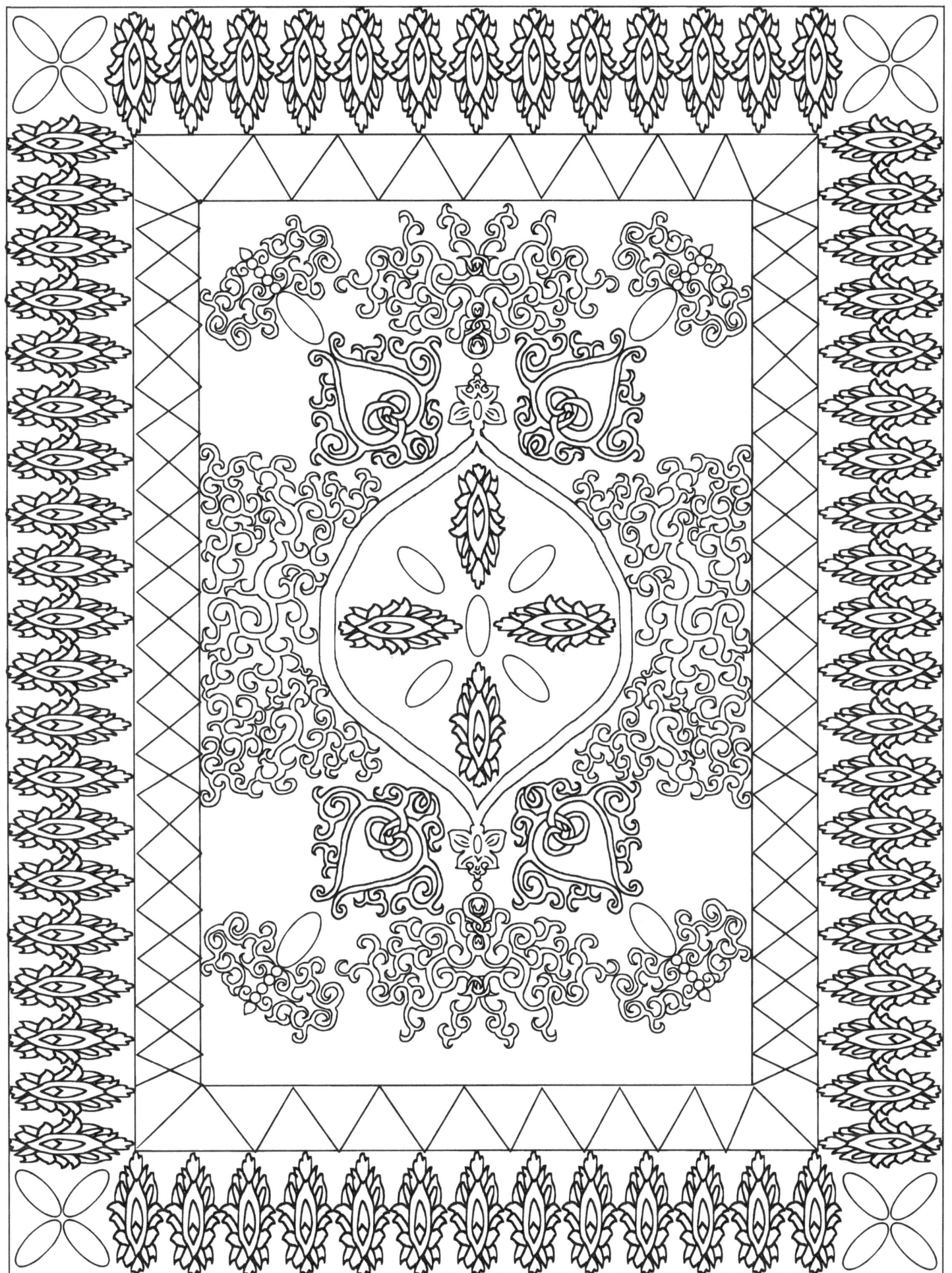

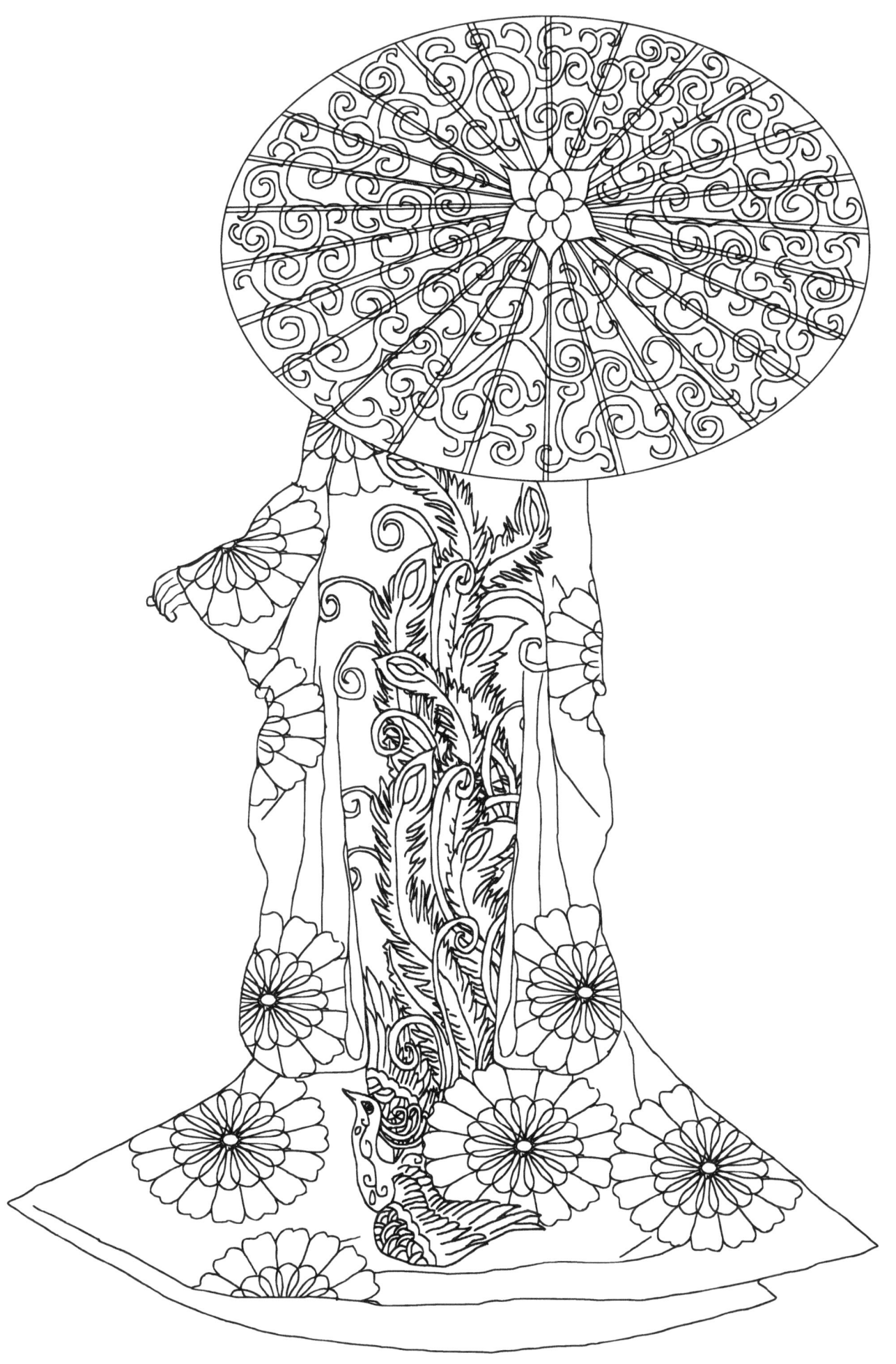

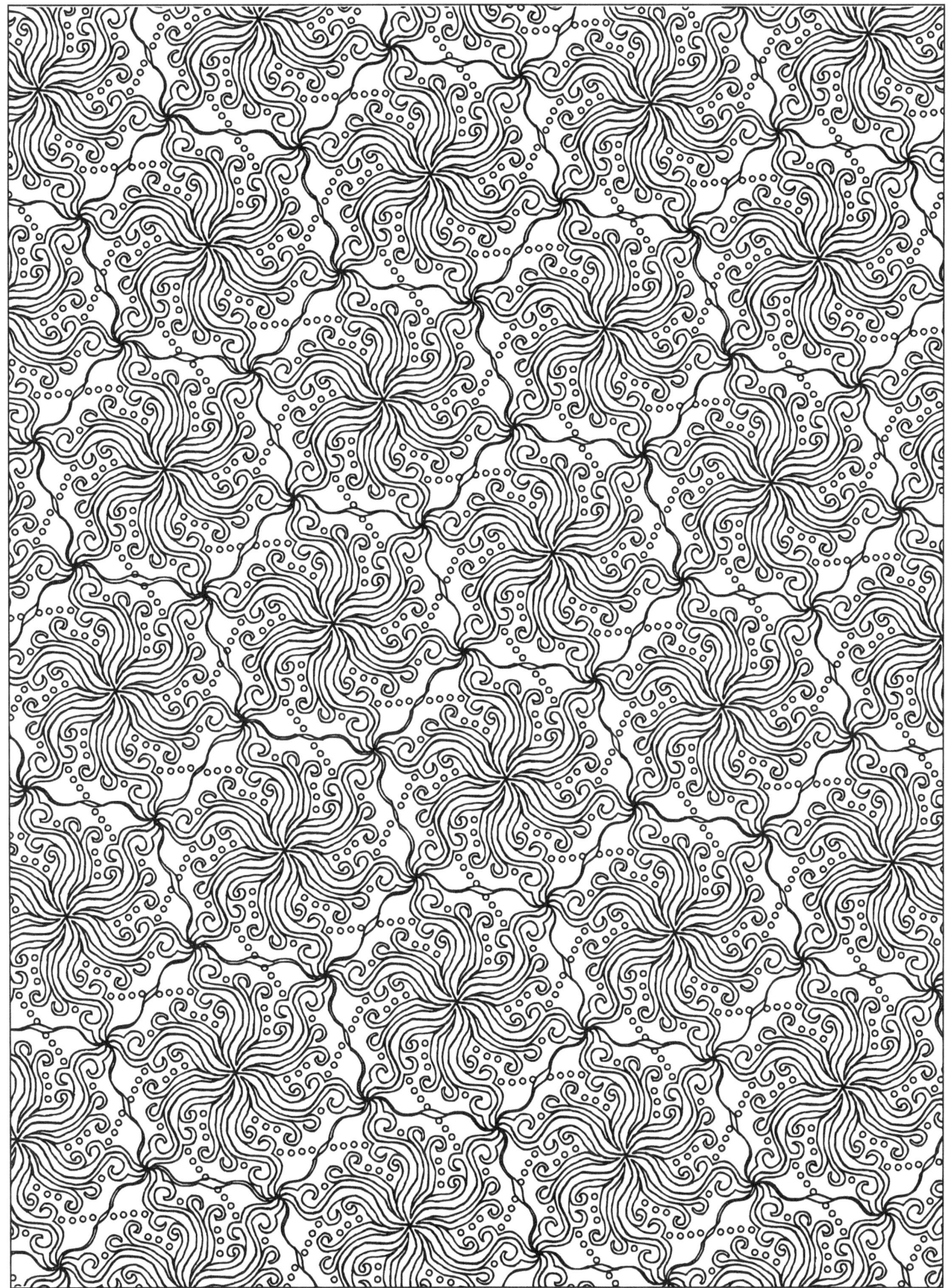

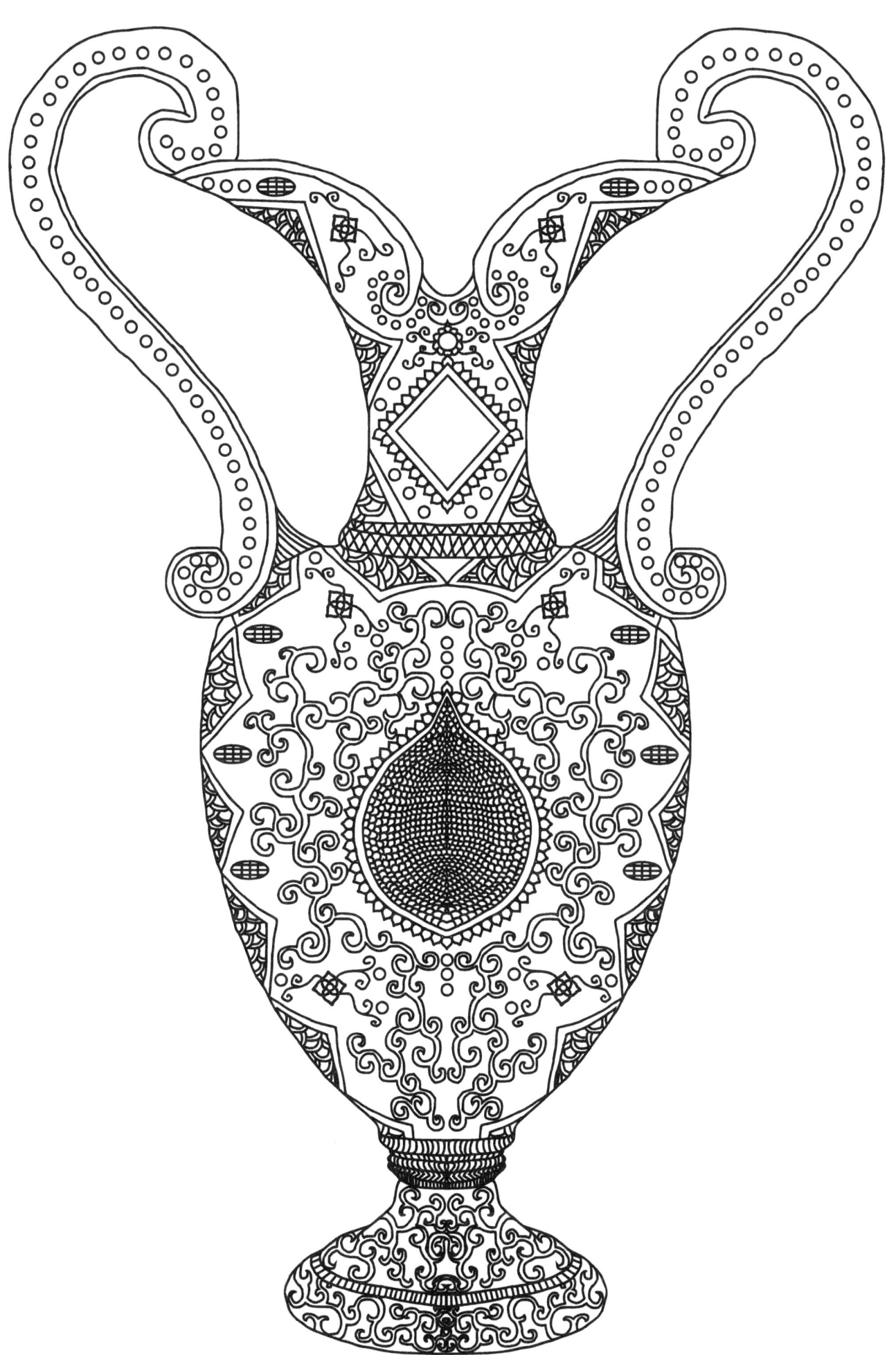

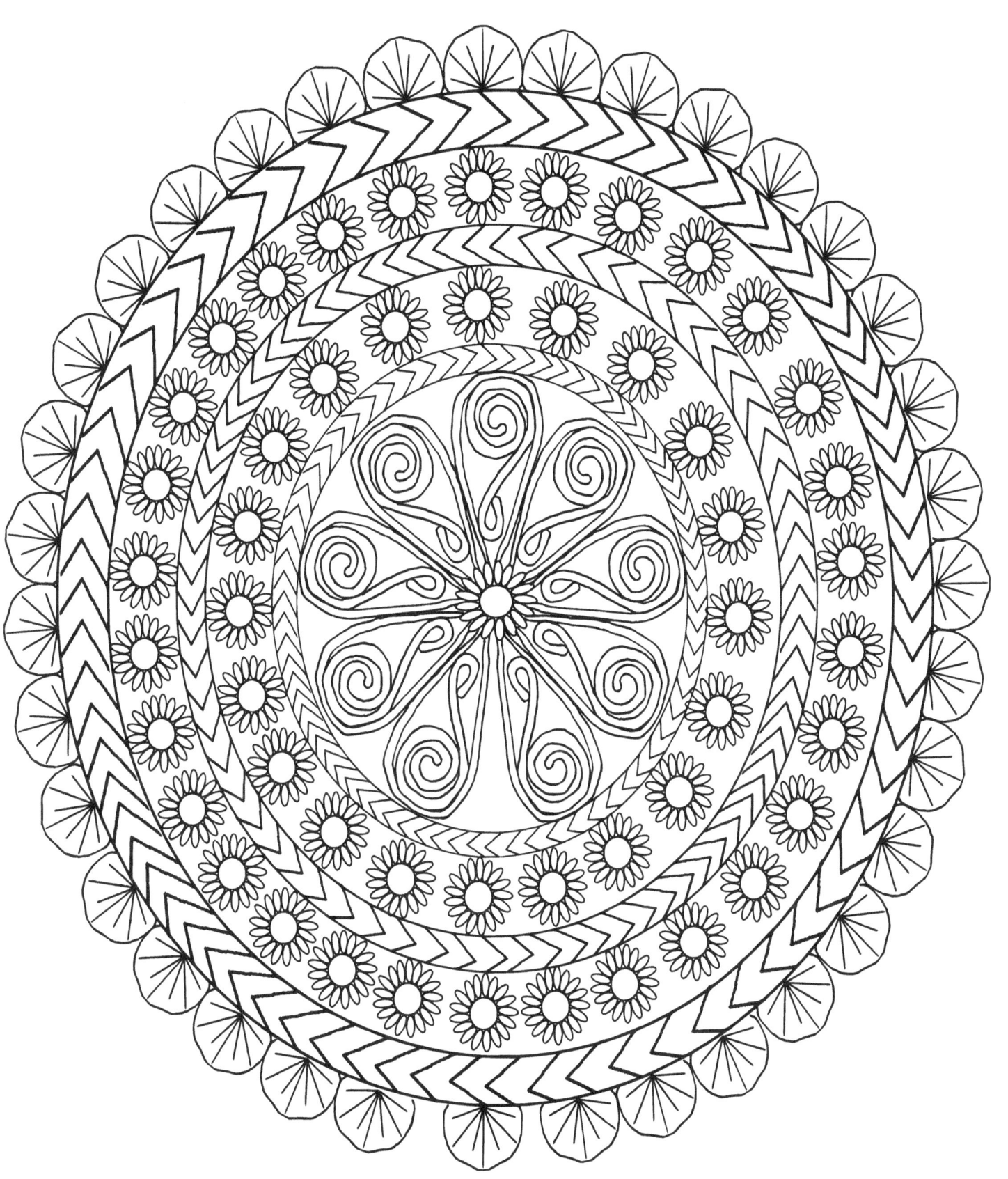